MINI
JERSEY

How to download your Free eBook

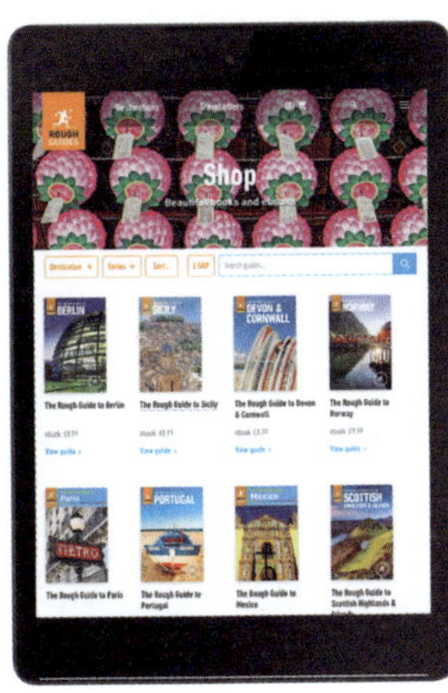

1. Visit **www.roughguides.com/free-ebook** or scan the **QR code** opposite

2. Enter the code **Jersey426**

3. Follow the simple step-by-step instructions

For troubleshooting contact: mail@roughguides.com

Contents

Introduction

Lying in the Bay of Mont St Michel, just 14 miles (22km) from the Normandy coast, Jersey has a distinct Gallic twist. The moment you arrive you have a sense of being abroad. Airport and harbour greet you with *Seyiz les beinv'nus a Jèrri* (Welcome to Jersey) in the French Norman patois, street and place names are still written in French, islanders are known as *crapauds* (toads) and every restaurant has a *plateau de fruits de mer*. Yet Jersey feels reassuringly familiar to UK visitors. Although it's not truly British, it has been linked with the British Crown for over 900 years, the official language is English, you drive on the left and cash machines dispense sterling. In other words, Jersey has the best of both worlds.

By the seaside at St Brelade's Bay

Tilting southwards, the island basks in the sun like a vast solar panel – Jersey has more hours of sunshine than anywhere else in the British Isles. The coastline offers a remarkable range of scenery from the vertiginous craggy cliffs of the north, to the Atlantic rollers of the windswept west, and the sweeping flat sands of the south. Along with its French flavour, the island offers all the ingredients of a traditional British seaside holiday: sandy beaches, crab-filled rock pools, big tides for beachcombing, picturesque fishing ports and ample family attractions. The sands of Jersey are washed by clear blue seas and the island has one of the largest tidal movements in the world. Twice a day waters retreat to reveal large expanses of golden sand or lunar-like seascapes, pierced with rocks and reefs. At low tide the island almost doubles in size – then the sea comes galloping in.

NOTES

Jersey may be a tiny speck on the map but the island has given its name to a breed of cow, a potato, a pullover, a lily, and a state in America.

The food here is a reason in itself to visit Jersey. The island has an impressively long list of outstanding restaurants, and plenty of simpler though equally excellent places to eat – and there's a wealth of fabulous local produce, including an exceptional bounty of freshly caught seafood.

In the unlikely event that you tire of the coast, Jersey packs in plenty of other attractions. Its tempestuous history has left a mark in monuments ranging from Neolithic tombs to castles, coastal towers and wartime tunnels and bunkers. With walkers and cyclists in mind, Jersey has developed a network of 'Green Lanes', where traffic is restricted to 15 mph (24kmph). Even on main roads the pace is slow, with a maximum speed limit of 40mph (64kmph). Inland Jersey is lush and pretty with wooded valleys, leafy lanes and pastures of doe-eyed cows.

But Jersey is no sleepy backwater. St Helier is a buzzing capital with a whole slew of knockout places to eat and drink; forts and follies have been converted to stylish self-catering complexes; and beach resorts offer a surge of adrenalin-fuelled sports. Walking and cycling have been encouraged – Jersey has an excellent network of cycle routes, and the coast path is an absolute stunner of a walk – although having said that the island still has one of the highest car ownership and user rates in the world.

'Peculiar of the Crown'

Neither wholly French nor English, Jersey has a quirky history and some unique, quasi-feudal customs. The Channel Islands are termed a 'Peculiar of the Crown', pledging allegiance directly to the English Crown, not to the parliament of the UK. As the last remaining territories of the dukes of Normandy, they toast the Queen of England as 'Our Duke of Normandy'. They are not full members of the EU – though when Britain joined (the EEC) in 1973, the Channel Islands were granted special privileges; and following Brexit when the UK departed from the EU, Jersey was left with a complex and finely balanced series of trade agreements to negotiate with both the UK and the EU. Jersey has its own government, legal

WHEN TO GO

The main tourist season on Jersey runs from April to October – although having said that, the island certainly has the potential to be a year-round destination, depending what it is you want from your holiday. July and August are the busiest months on the island, coinciding with the school holidays. Accommodation prices are at their highest, beaches at their busiest – but these are the months with the warmest temperatures (on land and in the water), and it's when some of the island's biggest festivals take place. The shoulder months (April to June and September/October) are the best time to visit – the weather is likely to be warm and sunny, there are fewer people and slightly lower accommodation prices than in the summer, ferry routes are up and running, and everything on the island will be open. April to June bring spring flowers, October brings autumn colours to the island. Winters, while undoubtedly wet, cold and at times stormy, are nevertheless milder than the UK – and at this time of year (with the exception of Christmas) you'll have the island largely to yourself, though the choice of accommodation and restaurants will be more limited since some close outside the main tourist season. Overall, January is the quietest month.

system and even its own non-uniformed honorary police force who have operated since Norman times and who alone can formally charge a suspect. The island prints its own currency and still has a £1 note (which went out of circulation in the rest of Britain in the early 1980s); it also issues its own stamps.

The clear waters of Portelet Bay

Size and Climate

Jersey may be the largest of the Channel Islands, but it is still a tiny island, measuring 9 miles (14km) long and 5 miles (8km) wide. Surprisingly it has a network of 350 miles (560km) of lanes, giving it the feel of a much larger island. The most southerly of the British Isles, Jersey has more daily hours of sun than anywhere else in Britain. In summer the island has a daily average of eight and a half hours of sunshine and an average maximum temperature of about 68°F (20°C). The best months to visit are from May to September, July and August being the hottest with temperatures often in the high 20s C (70s or 80s F). Sea temperatures are chilly or refreshing, depending on your hardiness, averaging 62.8°F (17.1°C) in summer.

The Bailiwick of Jersey embraces two offshore reefs Les Minquiers, commonly known as the Minkies, 9 miles (14km) south of St Helier, and Les Ecréhous, 5 miles (8km) off the north-east coast. In the past, French adventurers have occasionally attempted to take possession of the reefs and in 1950 the dispute over ownership was taken to the International Court in The Hague. The islands were awarded to Jersey – though French fishermen can still fish around the reefs.

Language

Until the Victorian era the common spoken language on the island was Jèrriais, a derivation of ancient Norman French. Large numbers of English settlers arrived on Jersey in the 19th century (many of them officers retired on half pay) and by the end of the century English was the prevalent language of St Helier. In all the country parishes, however, Jèrriais continued to be the main language until the 1960s. It is rarely heard these days but you might catch a few words from elderly locals in the countryside, perhaps at a market or agricultural auction. Only a handful of the population speak the patois fluently, but a concerted effort to revive interest in the language has led to the introduction of classes in some schools.

Jersey is great for cycling

Jèrriais never enjoyed the status of standard French, or what was referred to as *le bouôn français*. This was used in churches, law courts and administration and even today a few words are used for prayers before the States (or local government), court sittings and in official documents. Some

WHAT'S NEW

In 2024 Jersey launched its bid for UNESCO World Geopark status, gathering nominations from locals on what they felt should be included in the proposed site. The island certainly has a good case for Geopark status, with exceptional geology telling the story of how the island has been shaped by the action of time and tides. A new, free exhibition at the Jersey Art Museum takes visitors through the prosed Geopark. Starting in 2023, Jersey Heritage undertook major restoration work on Elizabeth Castle, the island's largest historical site – a project which remains ongoing. Hotel refurbishments and upgrades continue apace – recent reopenings have included the Grand Suite at the Grand Hotel and Spa. DFDS has taken over the ferry routes to Jersey from the UK and France from the previous longterm operator, Condor. Plans are also afoot to give both the airport and the Port Elizabeth ferry terminal a makeover, and in 2025 the government announced plans to completely redevelop the site of Fort Regent, a Napoleonic era fort which is currently home to an unforgivably ugly leisure centre.

street names in St Helier still have their original French names alongside the English ones given by 19th-century settlers from mainland Britain; eg, the somewhat prosaic Church Street was La Rue Trousse Cotillon – Pick Up Your Petticoat Street.

Economy

The economy saw major changes during the late 20th century as the financial services industry took over from agriculture and tourism. The financial sector is now completely dominant, and the skyline of St Helier has long ago seen a rash of high-rise HQs of banks, trusts, insurance and accountancy firms, along with a huge number of apartment blocks for financial workers. The Channel Islands have long attracted wealthy immigrants, seeking to benefit from the island's desirable lifestyle and advantageous tax laws. Only a handful are granted residency on Jersey each year through

Trail to St Ouen's Bay

the High Value Residency initiative. Among the criteria is sufficient wealth to create tax for the Jersey States in excess of £250,000, and an annual income of over £1.25 million.

The tourist industry took off after World War II when sightseers arrived to see the relics of the German Occupation. The island's unique position as a holiday island close to France yet English speaking, with well-run hotels and guesthouses, made it a holiday paradise from the 1950s. Tourism reached its peak in the late 1980s, then low-budget airlines and package holidays to more exotic climes led to a decline in tourism for the comparatively costly Channel Islands. The finance service industry which forged ahead in the 1990s stifled tourism. Hotels were demolished or turned into financiers' flats, and the number of visitors declined. The financial services industry now accounts for over 40 percent of the total economic activity on Jersey, employing over a fifth of the workforce. But tourism may be crucial in the future and in an effort to lure back the holidaymakers, particularly the younger ones, accommodation has been revamped, the sports and spa scene have been rejuvenated and gastronomy is thriving. The long downward trend in travel to Jersey was reversed in 2018 when the island saw the highest number of visiting holidaymakers since 2001. Although the COVID-19 pandemic in 2020 and 2021 halted the development of tourism for a time, visitor numbers were a very healthy 568,000 in 2024 – still about 75 percent of pre-Covid levels, but some 40,000 more than the previous year – and the aim is to see one million visitors by 2030. However the cost of travel, food and accommodation in Jersey are still high in comparison to the Med – and as sunny as the weather might be, it's competing with the likes of sunnier (and more affordable) Greece and Spain.

SUSTAINABLE TRAVEL

Jersey is a tiny island, and distances are short – so the first thing you can do to make your time there more sustainable and lower your carbon footprint is ditch the car. Jersey has a good, comprehensive bus network covering most of the places on the island you're likely to want to visit, and there's an equally well-developed network of cycle routes. Jersey is deservedly famous for its excellent seafood, but when eating out try to be aware of where the specific fish or shellfish you're ordering actually comes from. Whereas lobster and crab tends to be caught locally, and oysters are from the island's vast oyster beds, many fish are imported (cod, salmon, tuna and prawns for example are never from Jersey's waters). JP Restaurants has good information on what is, and isn't, local seafood (https://jprestaurants.com/news/where-does-your-fish-and-shellfish-come-from-in-jersey). There are also plenty of delicious vegetarian and vegan dishes on the menu at many of the island's restaurants. Finally, there are multiple options for reaching Jersey from the UK and France by ferry, always a greener option than flying.

10 Things not to miss

1 **MARITIME MUSEUM**
A first-rate museum that brings to life Jersey's former seafaring role, ideal for adults and children. See page 43.

2 **SAMARÈS MANOR**
A medieval manor renowned for its unique gardens and extensive range of plants. See page 54.

3 **JERSEY MUSEUM AND ART GALLERY**
Provides an excellent introduction to the history and culture of the island. See page 37.

4 **ELIZABETH CASTLE**
On guard at the great Tudor stronghold, which was once occupied by Sir Walter Raleigh. See page 45.

5 **JERSEY WAR TUNNELS**
An extraordinary complex of bomb-proof barracks constructed by the Germans. See page 47.

6 **NORTH COAST FOOTPATH**
The most exhilarating walk on the island, linking a chain of pretty bays such as Grève de Lecq. See pages 72 and 108.

7 **LA HOUGUE BIE**
One of the largest and best-preserved Neolithic passage graves in Europe. See page 51.

8 **BEAUPORT BEACH**
The islanders' favourite beach in a beautiful unspoilt bay. See page 64.

9 **JERSEY ZOO**
Renowned zoo established by Gerald Durrell in 1959 for the protection of endangered species. See page 81.

10 **MONT ORGUEIL CASTLE**
The stately symbol of the island dominates Gorey Harbour from its rocky promontory. See page 88.

A perfect day in Jersey

9AM

Breakfast. Indulge in a buffet breakfast in the Harbour Room of the Pomme d'Or Hotel in the heart of St Helier (Liberation Square) and enjoy views of the yacht marina across the square.

10AM

Picture-postcard harbour. Head out east from St Helier to Gorey, where a pretty harbour sits below the great medieval stronghold of Mont Orgueil. Climb the ramparts for magnificent views, stroll around the harbour and stop for coffee on the quayside.

NOON

Heading north. Explore at least a section of the majestic north coast, with its towering cliffs and perfect little fishing ports. Head north from Gorey via the B30 and B46, pass Gerald Durrell's famous Jersey Zoo , then dip down to quaint Bonne Nuit Bay, its tiny harbour sheltered by a single stone jetty.

12.45PM

Cliff walk. Pick up the cliff footpath eastwards in the direction of Bouley Bay to see some of the North Coast's most spectacular scenery. For lunch try the crab sandwiches or Thai specials at Bonne Nuit's café, overlooking the pretty bay.

2PM

St Aubin. Return to the south coast via the scenic Waterworks Valley and head east for St Aubin. Explore the port, browse in the Harbour Gallery arts and crafts centre, then head on west for St Brelade's Bay.

3.30PM

Afternoon relaxation. Relax on the beach here, take a dip or try your hand at blokarting or paddleboarding. If a quiet beach is more your scene, head a short distance west for the beautiful little bay of Beauport, reached down a bracken-covered cliff.

6PM

Corbière. It's only a short walk over a tidal causeway to Corbière Lighthouse, Jersey's most dramatic landmark. Watch the sun sink into the Atlantic.

7PM

Dinner options. Then enjoy gourmet fare at the Ocean Restaurant, Atlantic Hotel, with sublime views over St Ouen's Bay (book in advance). Cheaper options are pub grub with bay views at La Pulente in St Ouen's Bay, or the seafood cafés along St Brelade's Bay.

10PM

On the town. Back in St Helier spend a relaxing evening at the Royal Yacht Hotel, Weighbridge, right in the centre. Choose from bubbles in the P.O.S.H Bar or a nice quiet pint in the snug The Peirson. Alternatively just go with the flow in The Drift, a live music venue.

Jersey for foodies

8AM

Breakfast. Get your Jersey foodie tour off to a delicious start with breakfast at The Lookout, watching the waves roll in from a table beside the beach in St Aubin's Bay.

9AM

Central Market. Head into St Helier and pay a visit to the Central Market and the Fish Market on Beresford Street, where you'll find 40 independent specialist traders including fish and shellfish, and local fruit and veg.

9.15AM

Coffee. Grab a coffee and pastries at FOUR Artisan Bakery (see page 119), just around the corner from Central Market.

10.45AM

Wine tasting. Head out to La Mare Wine Estate, on the north side of the island (bus route 7). Join a guided tour of the vineyard, and settle in for a tasting experience – La Mare is Jersey's only vineyard, and along with white, red, rosé and sparkling wines, they also produce apple brandy and their own gin.

12PM

Lunch. Enjoy the best of Jersey's locally caught seafood at Jersey Crab Shack (see page 122) on the waterfront in St Brelade (bus 12 or 12a) – choose from the likes of fresh Jersey oysters, Jersey whole crab, Jersey crab linguine or fish of the day, or vegetarian options like South Indian butternut curry, and soak up the view of the bay from the terrace.

2PM

Gin tasting. Head back into St Helier and join a gin tasting, at Channel Islands Liquor Co. Tastings are held in the Old Sail Loft Distillery and last 1 hour, during which time you'll have the chance to taste a selection of their finely crafted gin, rum and vodka.

4PM

Foraging. Join a seaweed foraging tour off the southeast coast (bus route 1) with Jersey Walk Adventures; learn to identify edible seaweeds, and the dos and don'ts of collecting it. Tours last around 2.5 hours. There's usually at least one tour a month – if the dates don't work for you, join a tour of the oyster beds instead.

7.30PM

Dinner. You're spoilt for choice here, with outstanding restaurants like Awabi, Enotèca, Samphire and Tassili to choose from: but to complete a foodie-inspired tour of Jersey, it has to be the Michelin-starred Bohemia. Order à la carte or try one of the tasting menus (see page 118).

10PM

Cocktail. Enjoy a nightcap at The Blind Pig (1920s style decor) – or for a different ambience try The Don, The Melting Pot, or Project 52.

Hike the Jersey Coast Path

DAY ONE

St Helier to La Pulente. The Jersey Coast Path is a 48.5-mile (78km) loop around the island's spectacularly diverse coastline, blending easy walking with fantastic scenery and plenty of history, and no shortage of good places to stop for lunch (and for a swim). The walk can be comfortably spread over four days (or less), using St Helier as a base and getting to and from each stage by local buses. Start in St Helier and walk west around St Aubin's Bay, and stop for lunch in pretty St Brelade – The Crab Shack or Oyster Box are good choices (see pages 122 and 123). St Brelade is also one of the nicest beaches on the island. Then continue past Corbière Lighthouse (only walk out to the lighthouse itself if you've checked the tides) to La Pulente. Take the number 22 bus back to St Helier.

DAY TWO

La Pulente to Grève de Lecq. Take bus number 22 to La Pulente, then walk around the vast sweep of sandy beach that is St Ouen's Bay. Stop for lunch at Faulkner Fisheries, then it's up across the more rugged northwest corner of the island passing the Moltke Battery and other German relics from World War Two, Grosnez Castle and the beautiful sandy beach at Plemonte. Le Moulin de Lecq is a good place to stop for something to eat or a drink if you haven't already. Take bus 9 from Grève de Lecq back to St Helier.

DAY THREE

Grève de Lecq to Rozel. Return to Grève de Lecq on bus number 9. Follow the island's most spectacular stretch of coastline, along clifftop trails and passing Devil's Hole (a natural blowhole in the rocks), where you can follow a path down to take a closer look, and a viewing platform offers breathtaking views along the coast. Then continue past Sorel Point (from where there are yet more fantastic views). Stop for lunch at Bonne Nuit Beach Café, then walk past the pebbly beach at Bouley Bay (where Mad Mary's Beach Café is another well known place to stop for a bite), followed by more clifftop trails to Rozel. Take bus number 3 from Rozel back to St Helier.

DAY FOUR

Rozel to St Helier. The final, longest stage of the coast path takes you along the east coast, through patches of woodland and passing St Catherine's Bay, the Faldouet dolmen, and the dramatic Mont Orgueil Castle. Stop for lunch at The Seymour, a good local pub with tasty food and beers from Jersey's Liberation Brewery. Then round the southeastern tip of the island and walk past St Clement's Beach and Green Island Beach – depending on the tide, you can follow the beach to avoid the road here – and stroll back into St Helier.

History

Charming and laid back it may well be, but as a small island just off the coast of France, Jersey has seen a long and at times turbulent history. Striking reminders of its past are dotted all over the island, from the prehistoric burial grave at La Hougue Bie to coastal fortifications against the French, and the chilling Jersey War Tunnels from the German Occupation.

Little evidence was left by the earliest invaders but, from 1204, when King John lost Normandy to France and the Channel Islands chose to remain loyal to the English crown, successive defences were built against the invaders from France. The most recent fortifications date from the German Occupation in World War II when Hitler gave orders for the island to be transformed into 'an impregnable fortress'.

Prehistory

The earliest inhabited site on the island – and one of Europe's most important prehistoric sites – is La Cotte de St Brelade, a cave south of Ouaisné Bay, first occupied a quarter of a million years ago in the Lower Palaeolithic age. This sheltered site was inhabited intermittently for the next 200,000 years, but only during the colder months when the sea level was low enough to walk across from what is now France. The piles of woolly mammoth and rhino bones that were discovered at the foot of the 98-ft (32-m) cliff suggested that the cave-dwellers stampeded herds of animals over the cliff to their deaths. Archaeological investigations, which started here in 1881, and continued

NOTES

On rare occasions when the sands have been washed away by storms, you can see the remains of ancient tree stumps in St Ouen's Bay. These are the relics of an early Neolithic forest, probably dating from the time when Jersey was linked to the continent.

Dolmen entrance at La Hougue Bie

on and off until 1978, also brought to light 13 teeth belonging to a Neanderthal man or woman. The cave is closed to the public, but crucial relics are displayed in the Jersey Museum and the archaeological gallery at La Hougue Bie.

By 8,000 BC the climate was milder and Guernsey, Alderney and Sark had become islands. It was another two thousand years before Jersey broke away, and humans migrated here. Neolithic farmers established settlements from around 4,000 BC, clearing woodland and creating fields for crops and herds of sheep and cattle. The most conspicuous evidence of these settlers are the dolmens and menhirs scattered around the island. An outstanding example is the passage grave at La Hougue Bie (see page 51).

During the Bronze and Iron ages, the Channel Islands had trade links with Britain, Ireland and France – you can see an imported

5-ft (1.4-m) long gold torque from this era, discovered in St Helier, at the Jersey Museum.

The comparatively peaceful early Christian era was shattered by the Vikings who colonised Normandy. In 911 Rollo the Viking was made duke of Normandy on condition that he supported the king and protected the region from the invasions of other Vikings. The Duchy of Normandy expanded to the Channel Islands in 933 and the Normans made their mark with their feudal laws, seafaring traditions and language. An-oft quoted archaic Jersey law is the right to invoke *La Clameur de Haro*, a cry for justice said to be created by Rollo. If a civilian feels his property is being threatened he may go down on bended knee in the presence of two witnesses, and

Hermitage Rock, home of St Helier

ST HELIER – JERSEY'S PATRON SAINT

Born to pagan parents in Tongeren in modern-day Belgium, the hermit Helerius (or Helier) is said to have brought Christianity to Jersey. He arrived on the island in the 6th century, and founded a hermitage in a cave on a tidal islet where Elizabeth Castle stands today. For 15 years he devoted his life to prayer and to the protection of the small settlement of fishermen. In AD 555 Norman pirates landed on the islet, saw Helerius praying and cut off his head with axes – hence the two crossed axes on the emblem of St Helier. A monastery was founded here and Helerius was made a saint. His feast day is marked annually on the Sunday closest to 16 July by a pilgrimage to what is now known as Hermitage Rock.

cry: *'Haro! Haro! Haro! A l'aide, mon prince, on me fait tort'* (O Rollo! O Rollo! To my aid, my prince, I am being wronged'), followed by the Lord's Prayer in French. No further action or trespass can be taken until judgement is given in the appropriate court of law. The *Clameur* is rarely invoked today – the last time it was used successfully was in 1980. In 1994 a Jersey resident raised the *Clameur* against his brother in the Royal Square, but it was incorrectly invoked and therefore ignored. If the *Clameur* is used without justification the claimant is fined.

The British Connection

Following the victory of Norman Duke William II (William the Conqueror) at the Battle of Hastings, the Channel Islands became part of the Anglo-Norman realm. This was the beginning of the link with the English Crown, reinforced in 1204 when King John lost Normandy to France. The Channel Islands were given the choice of remaining loyal to the English Crown or reverting to France. They opted for the former, and in return the king granted them 'the continuance of their ancient laws and privileges', laying the foundation for self-government.

The French Threat

Fear of invasion from France led to the construction of coastal fortifications. In the early 13th century the great medieval fortress of Mont Orgueil was built to command the east coast, looking across to continental Normandy. 'Mount Pride' remained the chief stronghold of the island for nearly four centuries, but by the mid-16th century it was no longer up to defending the island. Work started on a new fortification on the islet of St Helier, built to withstand modern warfare and provide anchorage for the large merchant ships. Sir Walter Raleigh, who resided here as the island's governor, named it Fort Isabella Bellissima (Elizabeth the most Beautiful) in tribute to his beloved queen, Elizabeth I.

WWII German switchboard operator in the Jersey War Tunnels

During the English Civil War, Jersey hoped to remain neutral, but local rivalries led to the island's own brief civil war. The island finally emerged on the side of the king. The young Prince of Wales took refuge here briefly in 1646, and following the execution of his father, King Charles I in 1649, came back and was proclaimed King Charles II by the Governor of Jersey, Sir George Carteret. As a reward, Charles II bequeathed to Carteret a large tract of land in the American colonies, henceforth known as New Jersey. Jersey's loyalty to the monarch led to an inevitable invasion force of Parliamentarians under Cromwell. In 1651, 80 vessels crossed to Jersey with more than 2,500 troops under Admiral Blake. Royalist resistance was crushed and Cromwell's new model army controlled the island.

NOTES

The States of Jersey, the island's parliament, first convened in the 16th century. Today it comprises the Lieutenant Governor, who is the Monarch's representative in the island, the Bailiff, the Dean of Jersey, the Attorney General and the Solicitor General – along with 10 senators, 12 parish constables and 29 deputies.

Navigation and Knitting

Following the restoration of the monarchy Jersey enjoyed a phase of comparative peace and prosperity. Shipbuilders grew rich on cod-fishing in Newfoundland, splendid merchants' houses (known as 'Cod Houses') were constructed in St Aubin, while inland agriculture flourished. Cider was produced in large quantities and exported, sheep were abundant and the majority of the islanders (including men and children) were knitting stockings and fishermen's sweaters. (Legend has it that Mary Queen of Scots went to her execution wearing a pair of white Jersey stockings). Knitting in fact became so popular and lucrative that the harvest crops and seaweed collection began to suffer. A new law was introduced in

1708 forbidding the making of stockings during harvest and *vraicing* (seaweed collecting). Islanders were made to work on the land 'on pain of imprisonment on bread and water and the confiscation of their work'.

The Battle of Jersey

Jersey's privateering activities in the 1770s, when ships were licensed to plunder enemy vessels, led to two attempts by France to capture the island – first in 1779, and more famously, in 1781. On 6 January, under the command of Baron de Rullecourt, 600 troops took the island completely by surprise, landing at La Rocque in the southeast corner of the island and marching as far as Royal Square.

The Jersey Coat of Arms

The lieutenant-governor, still in bed, was tricked into believing that the enemy had around 14,000 troops, and immediately surrendered. However, a local 24-year-old officer, Major Francis Peirson, ignored the surrender and led the local militia to victory in the Battle of Jersey. Both Peirson and De Rullecourt were killed in action. This was the last attempt by France to capture the island. For fear of further invasions 30 Martello towers were constructed around the island, and many of these survive.

The Victorian Era

French vessels continued to be victims of Jersey privateers, leading to Napoleon's outcry: 'France can tolerate no longer this nest of brigands and assassins. Europe must be purged of this vermin. Jersey is England's shame'. With Napoleon's defeat at Waterloo, wars with France finally ceased. Although knitting and cider-making saw a decline, fishing, shipbuilding and agriculture still flourished. The prosperity of the island attracted newcomers, many of them army and navy officers retired on half pay after the Napoleonic Wars. By 1840 up to 5,000 English had settled here and by the end of the 19th century English had become the prevalent language of St Helier.

The German Occupation

The Channel Islands were the only British territory to fall into German hands during World War II. Tiny the islands may have been but Hitler saw them as the first step to his intended invasion of the United Kingdom. In 1940 Churchill decided that the islands, which had no strategic value for Britain, could not justify the cost of defence and the decision was taken that they should be demilitarised. Prior to the arrival of Hitler's troops 90,000 people fled the island while 80,000 decided to stay. Within two years Jersey was turned into an impregnable fortress, with thousands of foreign forced labourers and Russian prisoners-of-war toiling

Detail from Outbreak of War at the Occupation Tapestry Gallery

in harsh conditions to construct concrete walls, bunkers and gun emplacements, and over 11,000 German troops on the island. This was to be part of Hitler's Atlantic Wall project, a line of defence works extending all the way from the Baltic to the Spanish frontier. Over half a million tons of concrete were used around the coasts.

In the mistaken belief that an attack on the Channel Islands was imminent, Hitler gave orders for the construction of an emergency underground hospital for the treatment of German casualties – today's Jersey War Tunnels. Since the invasion never took place the hospital was never put to use. For the islanders the German Occupation was a time of hardship and deprivation, with shortages of food, fuel and medicines. During the last months the near-starving population was saved by the Swedish SS *Vega*, bringing Red Cross food parcels and other essential provisions. On 9 May

1945 British forces liberated the Channel Islands and the occupying forces surrendered peacefully. Citizens gathered to listen to Churchill's broadcast of the German capitulation: 'And our dear Channel Islands are to be freed today'. Liberation Day on 9 May has been celebrated ever since.

Postwar Developments

After the war, tourism was boosted by visitors from the UK, curious to see the after-effects of the Occupation. Tourism flourished up to the late 1980s, but has been stifled ever since by the finance industry. Stable government and advantageous tax laws led to the development of international financial services, including offshore banking, trust management and insurance. Today finance directly employs around 20 percent of the island's workforce and accounts for at least 40 percent of economic output.

More recently, in 2008 Jersey was rocked when an investigation into a children's home found evidence of years of abuse. In 2024, Jersey launched a public consultation as part of its bid to apply for potential UNESCO World Geopark status for the island. There are plans underway to modernise both Jersey Airport and Elizabeth Harbour. As the Channel Islands are not part of the EU, Brexit had no direct impact on their financial service industries and a limited impact on trade in goods.

Jersey is not part of the United Kingdom but a dependency of the British Crown, as it has been since 1204, with the islanders owing their allegiance to the Queen. The island is self-governing and has its own financial and legal systems and its own court of law. The island's parliament, known as the States of Jersey (see page 27), has been the subject of debate and argument for years. The introduction of ministerial government in 2005, adopted to replace the antiquated committee system, nevertheless left the States as divided as ever. In 2012 an Electoral Commission submitted a report on the composition of the States, with three potential recommendations for its reform. Voter turnout was somewhat lacklustre but a referendum was held in 2013, in which most voters opted for the proposal to reorganise the island into six large electoral districts, to reduce the number of States members slightly, and to allow parish Constables to continue to be members of the States.

Chronology

c.6,000 BC Jersey becomes an island when it is separated from Europe.

5,000–2,850 BC Neolithic Period. Megalithic tombs or dolmens are erected, including La Hougue Bie.

2,250–350 BC Bronze and Iron ages.

6th century AD St Helier is martyred by pirates in 555.

1066 Battle of Hastings. Channel Islands become part of the Anglo-Norman realm.

1204 King John loses Normandy to France but the islands remain loyal to the English Crown and are granted self-government.

1204 Work starts on Mont Orgueil Castle.

1550–1600 Construction of Elizabeth Castle.

1642–51 English Civil War. After a brief period of civil war, Jersey emerges on the side of the Royalists.

1649 Charles I beheaded. Charles II (then Prince of Wales) takes refuge in Jersey and is proclaimed king by the governor.

1651 Parliamentarians sent to put down Royalist resistance.

1781 Battle of Jersey. The heroic Major Peirson leads the local militia to victory when the French attempt to take over the island.

1940 Channel Islands demilitarised; 10,000 evacuated from Jersey.

1940–44 German Occupation. Foreign prisoners brought to the island to build defences. Rationing introduced.

1945 Liberation of the Channel Islands on May 9.

1973 Britain joins the EEC (now the EU).

1981 The hit BBC crime drama series *Bergerac*, set on Jersey, first airs. The series ran until 1991.

2004 Jersey celebrates 800 years of allegiance to the Crown.
2008 Haut de la Garenne, St Martin, becomes the focus of an ongoing investigation into historic child abuse.
2012 In the long-running issue of States reform, proposals are made to reduce the number of States Members.
2018 Channel Islands sign deal with UK over post-Brexit trade
2019 July temperatures break records in Jersey.
2020 The COVID-19 pandemic leads to Jersey's lockdown, with restrictions gradually lifted in 2021.
2024 Jersey launches public consultation into nomination of sites on the island for potential UNESCO World Geopark status.
2025 80th anniversary of Liberation Day.

Jersey Airport is preparing for redevelopment

Mont Orgueil Castle and Gorey Harbour

Places

Jersey is a tiny island of 9 miles (14km) by 5 miles (8km), but the network of 350 miles (560km) of roads, many of them narrow lanes, plus the speed limit of 40 mph (64km/h) and even 15 mph (24km/h) on some rural roads gives the impression it's far bigger. The island is divided up into 12 parishes – not that you would be aware which one you were in when driving or cycling around the island. Each parish has its own stretch of coastline, and wherever you are based on the island you are never far from a good beach.

The land slopes from the dramatic cliffs on the north coast to the flat sandy beaches of the south. The capital and hub of the island is St Helier on the south coast, which is the best centre for shopping and bus transport to attractions and beaches. However, you may prefer smaller, prettier and less traffic-thronged resorts such as Gorey or St Aubin – or the beach resort of St Brelade. If you don't have your own car these three centres all have good bus connections.

BEST PLACE TO TAKE PHOTOS

Start at **St Ouen's Bay**, where sweeping sands and Atlantic rollers compose dramatic sunrise and sunset shots. **Corbière Lighthouse** glows during golden hour – and its location on a tidal island is ideal for minimalist styles. Capture the morning pastel tones at **Gorey Harbour and Mont Orgueil Castle**, a perfect scene for a long exposure shot. Check weather apps to see if you can catch **St Catherine's Woods** in atmospheric mist, or go at dusk for chance to photograph bats and other wildlife. With its rows of fishing boats, **Rozel Harbour** offers a charming scene in all weather, as does the pretty **St Brelade's Bay Hotel**. From **Les Platons**, use a long lens to create compression of this birdseye island view, and go for a low-angle wide shot of **Elizabeth Castle** when it's low tide. Finally, explore the dramatic cliffs of **Grève de Lecq** – best in soft late-afternoon light.

The following pages start with St Helier and then take in some inland excursion destinations from the capital before going around the coast in a clockwise direction. Travelling from the south to north or north to south, often via picturesque valleys, is another option – but travelling east to west or vice versa is trickier unless you know the island well.

St Helier

Highlights

- **Liberation Square**, see page 37
- **Jersey Museum and Art Gallery**, see page 37
- **Parish Church of St Helier**, see page 38
- **Royal Square**, see page 39
- **Shopping streets and markets**, see page 41
- **Jersey Arts Centre and the Georgian House**, see page 42
- **Along the waterfront**, see page 43
- **The Waterfront Centre**, see page 44
- **Elizabeth Castle**, see page 45
- **Fort Regent**, see page 46

Capital of Jersey and its only real town, **St Helier** ❶ took its name from the hermit, Helerius, who arrived here in the 6th century, and a few years later had his head hacked off by Norman pirates (hence the axes on the flag of St Helier, see page 25). It was not until the 19th century that St Helier was developed as a main town with its harbours extended to become a commercial port. Today the first impressions are hardly picturesque. Arriving by sea you are greeted by a power station, cranes, high-rise blocks and traffic-thronged streets. However, the centre of the capital reveals a more charming side with its markets, museums and pedestrianised streets. A good starting point is the **Jersey Tourism** Visitor Centre (www.jersey.com) which is located within the Jersey Museum, in the town centre.

Liberation Square

It was in **Liberation Square** Ⓐ that crowds of islanders gathered on 9 May 1945 to welcome the British fleet that had come to release them after five gruelling years of German Occupation. The **Liberation Sculpture**, representing islanders and a British soldier clutching the Union Jack, was placed here in 1995, the fiftieth anniversary of the Liberation when Prince Charles opened the square. The Union Jack which featured in the original sculpture was then changed to a group of doves by the Occupation and Liberation Committee. Following comments about islanders being more likely to eat the doves than release them (food shortages were severe during the Occupation) the Union Jack was reinstated. On the north side of the square the **Pomme d'Or Hotel** overlooking the harbour provided a prime site for the German Naval Headquarters during the Occupation. On Liberation Day, in front of crowds of islanders, the Union Jack was raised on the balcony of the building, replacing the Nazi swastika.

Jersey Museum and Gallery

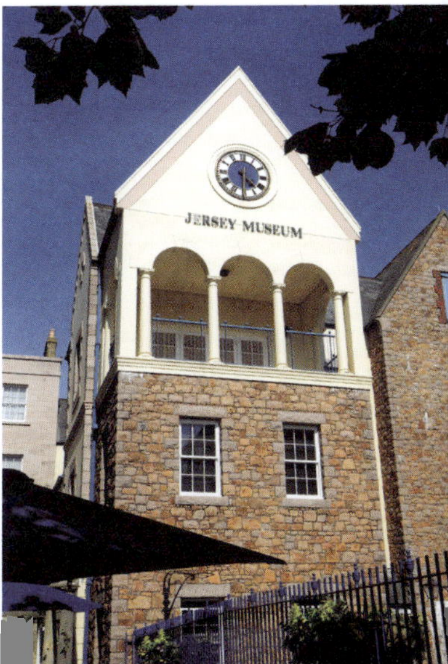

Jersey Museum and Art Gallery

Just east of Liberation Square, the **Jersey Museum and Art Gallery** Ⓑ (www.jerseyheritage.org) offers an excellent introduction to the island, tracing its story from prehistoric to present times.

THE JERSEY LILY

Two portraits of Jersey's most famous daughter, Lillie Langtry (1853–1929), herald the second-floor art gallery at the Jersey Museum. Born Emilie Charlotte LeBreton, daughter of a dean of Jersey, she married a wealthy widower, Edward Langtry, at the age of 21. They moved to London where she led the field in fashion and, on becoming the semi-official mistress of the Prince of Wales (later King Edward VII), the talk of the town. The portraits by Sir John Everett Millais, also a Jersey native, and Sir Edward Poynter, were both crowd-pullers at the Royal Academy in 1878 – a year after she had become the Prince of Wales' mistress. Lillie went on to become a highly successful actress – the first society woman to go on the stage. She took up American citizenship in 1897, divorced her husband, remarried and bought a ranch in California. She died in Monte Carlo and is buried in the graveyard in the church of St Saviour with the rest of her family.

On the ground floor you can see some fascinating archive footage of the early years of tourism on the island, and a reconstruction of a Paleolithic cave scene at La Cotte de St Brelade, where cave dwellers hunted animals by stampeding them off the clifftops. The first floor is devoted to the story of Jersey, and its culture and traditions, including oyster-catching, shipbuilding, farming, knitting and tourism. The most valued treasure is a Bronze Age flange-twisted torque, discovered in St Helier and thought to have been a gift from a tribal leader on the mainland to ensure the loyalty of an island chieftain. Adjoining the museum on the upper floors are the faithfully restored rooms of the Merchant's House, built in the 19th century for a wealthy merchant.

Parish Church of St Helier

Just north of Jersey Museum the **Parish Church of St Helier** **C** was a nerve centre of the town in times gone by. A church has stood here since the 11th century and it was a place where locals sought refuge in times of crisis, elections were held and bells were rung when enemy ships were sighted. Below the pulpit a memorial is dedicated to the heroic Major Peirson, who was killed in nearby Royal Square in the Battle of Jersey; his enemy, the Baron de Rullecourt, has a stone memorial in the graveyard. On the far side of the churchyard, Church Street still retains its fetching French-Norman name alongside the English. La Rue Trousse Cotillon or 'Pick Up Your Petticoat Street' dates from the times when ladies had to lift up their dresses to avoid mud, drains and sewers. The street leads into Library Place, where the aptly named Constable of St Helier, Pierre le Sueur, who founded the underground sewage system, is honoured with an obelisk.

Royal Square

East of Church Street the peaceful, leafy **Royal Square** **D** was formerly the hub of town life. This used to be the marketplace, and it was here that proclamations were announced, prisoners awaited trial in a wooden cage and petty offenders were flogged or put in the pillory or stocks. In 1648 two witches were strangled and burnt at the stake in the square. Happier events take place these days, such as weddings (for UK as well as Jersey residents) in the former corn market. In the centre of the square a stone

Statue of George II in Royal Square

commemorates the Battle of Jersey (see page 28) which took place here in 1871. The conspicuous gilded statue is King George II (1727–60), dressed as Caesar – but wearing the Order of the Garter. He was given this place of honour after donating £300 for the construction of St Helier's first harbour and the square's name was changed from the Market Place to Royal Square.

The king's coat of arms can be seen above the entrance of the **Royal Court**, the island's court of justice, on the south side of the square. On 8 May 1945 the bailiff of Jersey stood on the balcony here in front of a seething mass of islanders and relayed Churchill's message that the Channel Islands were to be freed. The **States Chamber**, Jersey's Parliament, stands to the left of the Royal Court. If you look carefully at the paving stones in the west half of the square you will see a large 'V' for Victory, which was secretly inscribed by a local stonemason while relaying the flagstones during the latter stages of the Occupation. Discovery of such acts of subversion would often lead to deportation, and he hid the 'V' under a layer of sand. The letters 'EGA' and '1945' were later added to commemorate the arrival of the Swedish Red Cross Ship, SS *Vega*. Both occupiers and islanders by this stage were near starvation but it was only civilians who

Inside the Central Market

were allowed the parcels from the ship. The Germans just watched as excited local people ripped opened their packets of cheese, chocolate and dried eggs.

Jewellers and 17th-century houses in Royal Square

Shopping Streets and Markets

From Peirson Place beside the pub you can access **King Street**, which, with **Queen Street**, makes up the main pedestrianised shopping thoroughfare. As well as the usual High Street chain stores there are individual retail outlets, including a remarkable number of jewellers. At Charing Cross at the western end a large metal *crapaud* (the symbolic Jersey toad) sits atop a granite pillar. The sculpture marks the site of an 18th-century prison and is engraved with the crimes and punishments of the time. At the other end of the street turn right for Halkett Place and the **Central Market** ❺ (https://jerseymarkets.je) on the other side of the street. A wonderful array of fresh produce – strawberries, asparagus, Jersey herbs and home-grown flowers – is laid out in this splendid Victorian glass-roofed building. The central feature is an ornate three-tiered fountain where cherubic figures lean on water jars with their paddles and goldfish swim in the pool below. Apart from fruit and vegetable stalls there are butchers and bakeries, a delicatessen and a dairy shop with products from the famous Jersey cow and other Jersey specialities such as *nier beurre* or black butter (see page 115).

For the **Fish Market** (also known as Beresford Market, same hours as Central Market) exit Central Market on the far side and turn left for Beresford Street. The building is modern without the elegance of Central Market, but there's a great spread of fresh fish, both local and imported. From Jersey waters you can expect to find live lobster, spider- and chancre crabs, scallops, locally farmed oysters and mussels, and amongst the fish, mackerel, wrasse and grey mullet. If all this looks tempting and it's time for a break, try out one of the two eateries here for a fishy snack and glass of wine.

Jersey Arts Centre and The Georgian House

At the end of Beresford Street you'll come face to face with a group of life-sized bronze Jersey cattle, including a calf looking suspiciously at a tiny *crapaud* or toad (the island mascot). Just to the north the **Jersey Arts Centre** F (www.artscentre.je) is a lively venue that hosts regular exhibitions of contemporary art, as well as concerts and theatre productions.

West of Central Market The Georgian House at **16 New Street** (www.jersey.com/things-to-do/attractions/listings/16-new-street-georgian-house-museum; charge) has been restored to its former elegance. Originally the home of a public notary, it has served as the headquarters of the Liberty Gentlemen's Club and the workshop of De Gruchy, the Jersey department store. By the 1980s it was

KINGDOM OF CONGERS

The firm oily meat of the conger eel was regarded as a delicacy, and it used to be salted, dried and preserved throughout the winter. The conger-rich waters and the popularity of the eel led to the island's nickname in the 17th century: the Kingdom of Congers. The eel was sold to the wealthy, while the poor fishermen were left with the bony head. This, however, was the key ingredient for a flavoursome fish soup, traditionally garnished with marigold petals.

neglected and demolition was threatened. However the National Trust bought the property for £1 in 2003 and thanks to a £1 million bequest it was able to undertake a meticulous renovation, and it is now open as a museum.

The Steam Clock

Along the Waterfront

On New North Quay, across the busy A1 from Liberation Square, the **Maritime Museum** ❻ (www.jerseyheritage.org; charge) occupies a 19th-century warehouse. This first-rate museum brings to life Jersey's former role as a seafaring state. It was one of the largest shipbuilding centres in Europe, its shipyards around the coast producing over 800 wooden sailing ships in the mid-19th century. It is very much an interactive museum where you can feel the force of the sea, sail a ship, tie a sheepshank and listen to songs and salty tales of the past. Among the highlights are a full-size replica of the bow of the Jersey-built brig, the *Orient Star*, and the Voyage Globe, a giant animatronic globe illustrating the journeys of Jersey's ships all over the world. On Mondays, Tuesdays and Wednesdays you can watch volunteer boat builders repair and maintain the museum's fleet of historic vessels. Examples of the restored boats can sometimes be seen in the marina outside the museum.

The museum shares the building with the **Occupation Tapestry Gallery** (same entrance ticket as the Maritime Museum). The

12 richly-coloured tapestries depict scenes of the German Occupation, from the announcement of war, through deprivation and deportation to the arrival of Red Cross parcels and Liberation. These finely worked panels were designed and stitched by the islanders to commemorate the 50th anniversary of Liberation, with each of the 12 parishes submitting a tapestry.

Next to the museum on the east side you are unlikely to miss the world's largest **Steam Clock**, modelled on a 19th-century paddle steamer. The benches here and around the old harbour basin record local vessels and their builders. Some of the ships sailed the oceans of the world, others worked the North Atlantic and the triangular trading routes based on the cod-fisheries, while the smaller vessels plied their trade in home waters.

The Waterfront Centre

The whole waterside area to the west is known as **The Waterfront Centre**. After years of political wrangling, this development is still not complete, and what has gone up so far has been hugely controversial. This vast space by the sea, with so much potential, intended as 'the new maritime quarter reconnecting the town with the seashore' and to 'breathe new life into the town and the island, enriching the quality of life of resident and visitor alike' has been ruined by utilitarian high-rise buildings, car parks, and a huge carbuncle of a hotel right on the water's edge (it actually won the 'prize' for the ugliest building built in the UK that year). The general feeling is that a huge potential has been sacrificed on the altar of the financial services sector, and that what could have been an attractive waterside, on the lines of other successful waterfronts in Europe, is doing little more than providing housing and parking for financiers. Development plans are ongoing. At the northern end **Les Jardins de la Mer** **H**, gardens with a fountain, bring some light relief, and the terrace of **La Frégate Café** provides fine views of Elizabeth Castle.

La Frégate, a distinctive waterfront café

Elizabeth Castle

Guarding the entrance of St Helier harbour, lies the great Tudor stronghold of **Elizabeth Castle** ❶ (www.jerseyheritage.org); charge), which defended the island for over 300 years. On an islet in St Aubin's Bay, the castle is connected to the shore by a causeway which you can cross at low tide. When the water is up the only means of access is the amphibious blue Castle Ferry (separate charge) which leaves at all tides from West Park slip (near Les Jardins de la Mer) and makes an enjoyable trip on a fine day.

By the late 16th century the great Mont Orgueil on Jersey's east coast was becoming increasingly vulnerable and a new fortification was required to meet the demands of modern-day warfare. Queen Elizabeth I ordered its construction and Sir Walter Raleigh, who lived here as governor, named it Fort Isabella Bellissima (Elizabeth the

Most Beautiful) after his queen. The fortification was expanded several times in the 17th century, though this didn't prevent it coming under fire from mortars during the English Civil War. Philip Carteret, the then-governor, sustained a siege here for 50 days and in 1651 a mortar shell attack by the Parliamentarians forced the Royalists to surrender. Charles II took refuge here on two occasions, once as Prince of Wales, and again, three years later, after the execution of his father, when he was proclaimed King Charles II. During World War II the Germans added to the fortification with bunkers, gun batteries and a command post at the top of the castle.

Visitors can explore the battlements and bunkers, climb up to the oldest fortress of the Upper Ward and discover **Hermitage Rock**, home of St Helier, Jersey's patron saint (see page 25). Buildings around the Parade Ground house exhibitions covering the history of the garrison, the development of the cannon and the story of the Jersey Royal Militia. On regular days throughout the season history is kept alive by displays of artillery, military parades and the firing of the noonday cannon. There is plenty of audience participation and visitors may be dragooned into drill practice and marching the Parade Ground!

Elizabeth Castle at high tide

Fort Regent

The final fortress built on Jersey was **Fort Regent** ❶,

whose location is marked by the white spaceship-like dome above the town and visible from Elizabeth Castle. Fears of further French invasion led to its construction in 1806–14 but it was never needed to defend the island. The building was converted into a huge leisure centre in 1958 with sports facilities, concert hall, exhibitions and entertainment. Today it offers a PlayZone for children, a sports club and occasional concerts and events. Plans were unveiled in 2025 to completely redevelop the site by 2028.

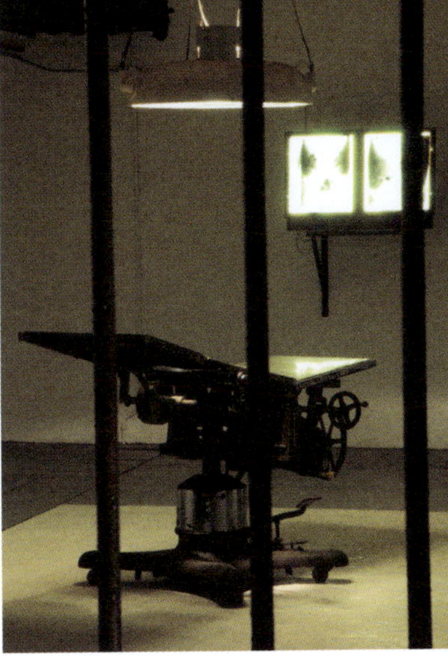

Operating theatre at the Jersey War Tunnels

Excursions from St Helier

Highlights

- **Jersey War Tunnels**, see below
- **Hamptonne Country Life Museum**, see page 49
- **Orchid Foundation**, see page 50
- **La Hougue Bie**, see page 51
- **Samarès Manor**, see page 54

Jersey War Tunnels

Following the Führer's orders to turn the Channel Islands into 'an impregnable fortress', slave workers were put to work on creating command posts and gun emplacements around the island. The most evocative of all these German fortifications is the **Jersey War Tunnels** ❷ (Les Charrières Malorey, St Lawrence; www.jerseywartunnels.com; charge), the vast underground complex of Ho8 (Höhlgangsanlage 8). By car, take the A1 west out of St Helier, turn right on to the A11 at Bel Royal, then follow the signs for the War Tunnels. Alternatively you can take Liberty Bus Route 8 or 28 both from Liberty Bus Station, St Helier (www.libertybus.je). You can also cycle to the tunnels, following Cycle Route 4 which leads north from the waterfront of St Aubin's Bay (www.jersey.com/holidays/active/cycling).

Hundreds of forced labourers from all over Europe, including Russian and Polish prisoners-of-war, were used to create a complex of bomb-proof barracks to protect the garrison of around 12,000 men against assault from sea or air. The project involved 16 tunnels, requiring the excavation of thousands of tonnes of rock and 6,000 tonnes of concrete to line the tunnels. Work came to a halt in 1943 when news came through of an impending Allied invasion of Europe, and orders were given for the complex to be turned into a huge subterranean casualty clearing station. The wards, operating theatre and administrative rooms were to cater for hundreds of wounded. The allied landings never happened, the German forces surrendered peacefully on 9 May 1945 and the unused Ho8 was taken over by a British medical unit and virtually stripped of all its contents. A year later it opened to sightseers and souvenir-seekers.

Hospital scenes within the long, dark and chilly tunnels have been reconstructed and a combination of archive film footage, islanders' reminiscences, photos and poignant correspondence chart life under the Nazis. The exhibits bring home the hardship endured by slave labourers (at least 560 died in the Channel Islands), the deprivation of islanders and the fate of those who were deported to camps in Germany. The site also incorporates

Garden of Reflection at the War Tunnels

the **Garden of Reflection**, designed for visitors to contemplate the suffering during the Occupation; and the **War Trail**, covering land once used as an artillery battery, and now being reclaimed by nature.

Hamptonne Country Life Museum

In the heart of rural Jersey is the **Hamptonne Country Life Museum** ❸ (La Rue de la Patente, St Lawrence; www.jerseyheritage.org; charge), which takes you back to farming life as it was three centuries ago. The most scenic route there is via **Waterworks Valley**: follow the A1 from St Helier until you are about half way round St Aubin's Bay, then turn inland at the C118. A refreshing antidote to frenetic St Helier, this is a peaceful green valley whose streams used to power six watermills. Today the island's main

The 'goodwyf' at Hamptonne Country Life Museum

reservoirs are located here; beyond the Dannemarche Reservoir, fork left on to the C119 for the museum. Cycle Route 2 will also get you to the museum from St Aubin's Bay, or it can be reached by bus No 7.

A cluster of farm buildings has been faithfully restored and there are meadows, woodland and orchards to explore. Two houses have been recreated to demonstrate the living conditions of farming families in the 17th and 18th centuries. Expect a spinner, lacemaker, blacksmith or a 'goodwyf' in period costume who will tell tales of the English Civil War or entertain you with local gossip from the old farming community. The refurbished Syvret House gives an insight into 1940s rural life including farming traditions, day-to-day family life, language, religion and the German Occupation. The nearby cider barn houses the apple crusher and twin-screw apple press that are still used every autumn to make cider. Children can meet the Hamptonne pigs, feed the chickens, follow a nature trail or test their knowledge with activity sheets or puzzles – or you can order a picnic to enjoy in the orchards or meadows (call in advance).

Orchid Foundation

Horticultural enthusiasts should not miss the **Eric Young Orchid Foundation** ❹ (Victoria Village, Trinity; www.ericyoungorchid.

org; charge) which displays an award-winning collection of orchids within a purpose-built nursery and exhibition complex. The late Eric Young first established his collection in Jersey in 1958 and within a decade it was recognised as one of the leading private collections in Europe. The complex features permanently planted landscapes that use raised beds, traditional Jersey granite, logs and branches to show the orchids in all their splendour. The nursery is not a commercial outfit, but there are often a few orchids for sale.

La Hougue Bie

One of the largest and best-preserved Neolithic passage graves in Europe, **La Hougue Bie** ❺ (La Route de la Hougue Bie, Grouville;

One of the Hamptonne rooms used in filming Under the Greenwood Tree

Award-winning orchids

www.jerseyheritage.org; charge) has been a centre of activity for 6,000 years. To get there by car, take the A6 or A7 from St Helier to the Five Oaks roundabout, then turn right on to the B28 and follow the signs for La Hougue Bie. La Hougue Bie is on cycle routes 3 and 8 (though bizarrely it's not labelled clearly on the Jersey cycle map). It is also served by bus Nos 13 and 21. If on arrival you're wondering where the monument is, head for the huge grassy mound. This conceals a rubble cairn which was built on top of the dolmen and faced with dry-stone walling. Centuries later Christianity made its mark on the site by the construction of two little chapels on top of the mound.

Following the Reformation the site passed into private hands and Philippe d'Auvergne, the duke of Bouillon, converted the ruined chapels into a neo-Gothic folly that became known as The Prince's Tower. A hotel was added in the 19th century and the site became one of the island's first tourist attractions, complete with pleasure garden, bowling alleys and fine views. Excavations in 1924 necessitated the demolition of the hotel and tower and led to the discovery of a low passage leading to funeral chambers.

The roof height of the tunnel-like passage grave is only 5ft (1.4m), so you have to stoop to gain access to the funereal chamber. Built of huge blocks of stone topped by capstones, this dark, mysterious – and far from spacious – chamber would have been used for ritual and ceremonial functions, as well as for burials. Fragments of human and animal bones, along with flint arrowheads and pottery fragments, were discovered here during excavation. Limpet shells were found on top of the capstones; these could have had a religious significance – or they might have just been the leftovers from the dolmen builders' lunch.

A pathway leads up to the two restored chapels at the top of the mound. The **Chapel of Notre Dame de la Clarté** (Our Lady of the Dawn) was built in the late 12th century in alignment with the dolmen, suggesting that its Christian creators recognised the link between the ancient monument and the equinoctial alignment. In

Dolmen entrance, La Hougue Bie

NOTES

In the 1520s Dean Mabon, who had made a pilgrimage to the Holy Land, had a shrine built under the Jerusalem Chapel in imitation of the Holy Sepulchre in Jerusalem. According to a Protestant chronicler of the late 16th century, the dean claimed to receive visions of the Virgin Mary and staged fake miracles to encourage alms from pilgrims.

the 1520s Dean Mabon (see box) added what became known as the **Jerusalem Chapel**, where, if you switch on the lights, you can see the faint outlines of two archangels.

During the Occupation in World War II a battalion command bunker was built on the Hougue Bie site, beside the burial mound. This now houses a memorial to the workers who were brought to the Channel Islands from Europe to work on the German fortifications, which is particularly moving. In one section the words of the slave labourers and their guards are recorded on metal plaques; in another the names of 503 victims are inscribed on a glass pillar.

Also on the site are galleries of geological and archaeological displays, highlights of which are animal remains from La Cotte de St Brelade (see page 22), jadeite axe-heads that were traded across to Europe in 3000 BC, and rare hordes of Iron and Bronze Age coins.

Samarès Manor

Fourteen acres (6 hectares) of gorgeous landscaped gardens are the highlight of **Samarès Manor** ❻ (www.samaresmanor.com; charge) in St Clement's, southeast of St Helier (access either by car, cycle route 1 or bus No 1a). The name Samarès derives from the old Norman French *Salse Marais*, or saltwater marsh, dating from ancient times when the owners profited from the saltpans on the low-lying land to the south. The grounds were originally designed in the 1920s by Sir James Knott, a shipping magnate and philanthropist, who spent the last 10 years of his life here. Knott's passion was plants from the East, hence the Japanese Garden, Exotic Border, rock and water gardens and large ponds with islands and camellia plantations.

Bordering the manor house is a delightful walled garden full of culinary, cosmetic and medicinal herbs. The former bring flavour to dishes served in the Herb Garden Café (also good for cream teas). Plants in the gardens with a red marker can be purchased and taken back to the UK. The nursery has been expanded and offers a good choice of plants for sale. Samarès specialities are roses, herbs, hardy perennials and lavender – as well as favourites such as the Jersey agapanthus, ice plants and Echium (bee plants). Visitors can take a guided tour of the manor (charge) and the **Jersey Rural Life Museum** (free).

Samarès Manor is surrounded by extensive gardens

The Southwest

Highlights

- **St Aubin's Bay**, see below
- **St Aubin**, see page 58
- **Noirmont and Portelet**, see page 59
- **Ouaisné and St Brelade's Bays**, see page 61
- **Churches of St Brelade**, see page 62
- **Jersey Lavender Farm**, see page 63
- **Beauport**, see page 64

From St Helier a vast crescent of south-facing sands extends all the way to the picturesque port and resort of St Aubin's in the west. A headland with glorious bay views divides the port from St Brelade, where palm-fringed gardens overlook one of the finest beaches on the island. From here you can walk along the clifftops to the dramatically located Corbière Lighthouse. Cyclists, joggers or walkers can cover the southwestern corner of the island by following the route of the old Jersey Railway line. Opened in 1870, this ran from St Helier to St Aubin, following the bay, and was then extended to Corbière. The track was turned into a footpath after competition from buses led to the closure of the railway and in 1936 fire destroyed much of the rolling stock at St Aubin.

St Aubin's Bay

Stretching from Elizabeth Castle to St Aubin, the bay is a long sweep of sheltered, unbroken sands. During spring tides the water laps the seawall, then retreats over 300m to expose a huge expanse of flat sands – so flat and expansive it was used for take-off and landings of De Havilland Dragons before Jersey's airport opened in 1937. St Aubin's is not the prettiest of the island's beaches, and it's a long trek through shallow waters to swim, but the sea is normally calm and safe for children and water sports are plentiful.

The beach between West Park and First Tower was once the site of the island's largest shipbuilders. In the 1860s Jersey was one the largest ship-building centres in the British Isles, employing hundreds of workers. Further west, halfway round the bay on the A1 inland, St Matthew's Church at Millbrook is known as the **Glass Church** (free). The austere-looking church was built in 1840 but only attracted attention after the Parisian glass designer, René Lalique, embellished its interior in 1930s. He was commissioned by Lady Trent as a memorial to her husband, Jessie Boot, of Boots the Chemist. Panels, pillars, windows, the altar cross and the Art Deco angels are all rendered in opalescent glass, giving a soft glow to the church interior.

Portelet Bay viewed from Noirmont Point

St Aubin

You wouldn't think it now but **St Aubin** ❼ was the island's commercial hub from the early 16th to the 18th centuries. Fishermen used to set off from here in small boats to cross the Atlantic in spring, returning in autumn with rich stocks of Newfoundland cod. The fish was dried and salted, then shipped to the Mediterranean and Central America, to be traded for wines, spirits and tobacco. Merchants who made fortunes from fishing and shipbuilding built grand four-storey houses (known as 'cod houses') along the shore or in steep narrow streets, some of which you can still see today.

Named after the 5th-century Bishop of Angers, protector against piracy, St Aubin ironically also acquired much of its wealth through profiteering during the English Civil War. Jersey was pro-Royalist and the local ships were licensed to capture boats belonging to the enemy. Booty from these attacks was stashed away in the Old Court House Inn overlooking the harbour, now a historic hotel and restaurant. The building may look familiar to *Bergerac* fans – it featured as The Royal Barge in the cops-and-robbers series back in the 1980s (rebooted in 2025).

St Aubin and its harbour

St Aubin today is a picturesque port, popular for its villagey atmosphere, seaside strolls and ample

View of St Brelade's Bay from Portelet Common

choice of quayside eateries. At low tide you can walk out to **St Aubin's Fort** (closed to the public), originally built in the 1640s to ward off French invaders and extended over the centuries. The last to leave their mark on the fort were the Germans during the World War II Occupation.

Noirmont and Portelet

A steep hill from St Aubin (A13, or if you're cycling take cycle route 1) takes you through a wooded valley west towards St Brelade's Bay. Just after the hairpin bend you would have once been able to admire the **Shell Garden** which its owner the late Colin Soudain decorated with thousands of seashells from the 1950s onwards – it was left as a gift to the island, but sadly in 2015 the National Trust nevertheless sold it to a local businessman, who demolished it.

The next left turn brings you south to **Noirmont Point** ❽, a windswept headland, once known as Niger Mons or Black Hill, after the dark clouds that gather here. Sitting on the clifftop is a huge German command bunker (occasional openings, check www.cios.org.je), extending to a depth of 40ft (12m) on two floors with a large observation tower. Views from here encompass St Aubin's Bay and on a really clear day you can spot the coast of Brittany on the horizon.

To the west lies **Portelet Bay** ❾ an inviting beach with soft sands and a sheltered setting, accessed down a long flight of steps from the clifftop car park at the Old Portelet Inn. The offshore Ile au Guerdain, topped by a defensive tower, became known as Janvrin's Tomb after an unhappy episode in its history. Janvrin was a sea captain who was refused landing at St Aubin's harbour when returning from plague-infested Nantes in Brittany in 1721. Janvrin then fell victim to the plague, and had to be buried on the island. His body was later transferred to St Brelade's cemetery. The tower on the islet was built over the grave in 1808 as one of the many fortifications against possible invasions during the Napoleonic Wars.

NOTES

Portolet Bay – or rather, a series of proposed development projects which threatened to have a hugely detrimental impact on this and other fragile stretches of the island's coastline – was the catalyst behind the formation of Jersey National Park. Some 7,000 islanders gathered in protest on the beach at Portolet Bay in October 2009, forming a human chain which stretched from Le Braye almost to L'Etacq. Jersey National Park (https://jerseynationalpark.com) was created two years later, covering a large part of the island's coastal areas – some 2,145 hectares, or 16 percent of the island's surface, within which any proposed development is strictly controlled.

Ouaisné and St Brelade's Bays

Portelet Common, west of Portelet Bay, covers 77-acres (31-hectares) and is set on the clifftop, affording dramatic sea views across to St Brelade's Bay. Below the slopes on the north-facing side of the common lies La Cotte de St Brelade (closed to the public), a major Palaeolithic site (see page 22). To the west, sea views stretch to the far end of St Brelade's Bay. Below is **Ouaisné Bay** (prounounced 'Waynay'), a spacious, sandy beach (accessed by a steep path from the common or by road) which is rarely crowded, even in midsummer. Behind the beach, the gorse-covered common is home to some rare species of fauna, including the Jersey green lizard, the agile frog and the Dartford warbler – though you would be lucky to spot them.

The Perquage from St Brelade's to the harbour

St Brelade's Bay ⓾ lies beyond the rocky promontory and is accessed across the beach at low tide, or over the rocks when the water is up. This is justifiably Jersey's most popular beach resort: a large crescent of gently sloping, southern-facing sands, with clear blue waters and water sports galore. You can choose from blokarting (also called sand karting), stand-up paddle boarding, kayaking, coasteering, bodyboarding, windsurfing, water-skiing, dinghy sailing, skim boarding, surfing and paddle surfing. Above the bay, a boardwalk is flanked by cafés, restaurants and bucket-and-spade

Fishermen's Chapel

shops. Neat and colourful palm-lined gardens border the promenade while the slopes behind are dotted with the immaculate mansions of multimillionaires.

Churches of St Brelade

Away from the crowds at the far west of the bay, the parish **Church of St Brelade ⓫** overlooks the tiny harbour. The large churchyard was formerly the burial place of more than 300 Germans, some of whom had been prisoners here in World War I, others who had served during the more recent German Occupation. The bodies were exhumed in the early 1960s and given a final resting place at a military cemetery in St Malo across the water. The pink granite church dates back to the 11th and 12th centuries and still retains Norman features. If the lights aren't on, there's a switch tothe left of the entrance. The enchanting interior has warm granite walls, with beach stones and limpet shells embedded within them.

Just next door to the church is the lovely **Fishermen's Chapel** ⓬ also built of local granite and dating back to Norman times. Following the Reformation it fell into disuse for some 300 years, and was variously used as an armoury, store room and carpenter's shop. Restoration in the early 20th century revealed a series of medieval frescoes depicting scenes from the Old and New Testaments. Only fragments remain but information boards fill in the gaps so you can make out the scenes. The most complete and the oldest fresco is the *Annunciation* on the east wall, which includes the members of the donor's family kneeling on either side of the Virgin and Archangel.

Jersey Lavender Farm

Follow your nose inland from St Brelade's Bay for **Jersey Lavender** ⓭ (Rue du Pon Marquet, St Brelade's; www.jerseylavender.co.uk; charge), whose 9 acres (3.6 hectares) of sweet-scented lavender resemble a little patch of Provence. The garden contains around 80 different varieties of lavenders, plus more than 100 kinds of culinary, medicinal, aromatic and dyers' herbs. The lavender is cut by hand, distilled on site and the essential oils matured and blended with other ingredients to produce soaps, lotions, fragrances, lavender bags and more. A video presentation shows all the stages of production and in summer there are tours of the farm. The best time to visit is between early June and late July/early August when the lavender is in flower, before it's all harvested. Lavender products are on sale in the shop – for a list of all the therapeutic usages of lavender oil, go to the website – and for all-day refreshments and home-made cakes, try Sprigs Café next to the shop.

PATH TO FREEDOM

The granite stairway from St Brelade's churchyard to the tiny harbour is one of the last remaining sections of a Perquage, or sanctuary path. In the pre-Reformation era criminals who sought refuge in a parish church and swore to leave the island and give away all their possessions could use one of the Perquage walks, which linked each parish church to the sea. From there they would take a boat and seek sanctuary in France. The Perquages ceased to exist in 1683 when King Charles II bequeathed them to Sir Edward de Carteret, Viscount of Jersey, who then sold the land to farmers who owned the neighbouring fields.

Beauport

The steep road westwards from St Brelade's Bay takes you to **Beauport** ⓮ the islanders' favourite beach. Hidden away from the main road, entailing a longish trek down a steep hill, this beautiful sheltered bay is totally unspoilt. The waters here are crystal-clear, the soft sands washed by the tides and free frombeach facilities. There is not even a drinks kiosk, let alone parasols – so remember to take your own provisions, along with sun cream.

The West Coast

Highlights

- **La Corbière**, see below
- **St Ouen's Bay**, see page 66
- **Channel Islands Military Museum**, see page 68
- **L'Etacq**, see page 69
- **Grosnez Castle**, see page 71

This is Jersey's wildest coast, with waves crashing around Corbière Lighthouse and Atlantic surf pounding the huge beach of St Ouen's. This 4-mile (6.5km) arc of sand stretches almost the entire length of the west coast. Behind the beach a large expanse of unspoilt sand dunes is home to a wealth of flora and fauna.

La Corbière

Sitting atop the jagged rocks, **Corbière Lighthouse** ⓯ is one of Jersey's most familiar landmarks and a favourite spot from which to watch sunsets and rough seas. The name Corbière derives from *corbeau* (crow), traditionally seen as a bird of ill omen, and this wild and desolate tip of the island is inextricably linked with tales of shipwrecks and smuggling. The first recorded ship to flounder on the rocks here was a Spanish vessel in 1495 carrying a cargo of wine. The seigneur of St Ouen was entitled by Jersey law to shipwrecked vessels and their cargo, and it is said that smugglers worked alongside the seigneur, luring ships on to the treacherous rocks with lanterns, which looked like the lights of vessels on the open sea. Among other casualties at Corbière was the Royal Mail Steam Packet, which was shipwrecked on the rocks in 1859. A lighthouse was finally erected here in 1874 – the first one in the British Isles to be made of reinforced concrete rather than stone. Weather permitting, the light beam can be seen from a distance of up to 18 miles (29km). The lighthouse is closed to the public.

At mid to low tide you can cross the causeway to the lighthouse, but check the tides before doing so and heed the siren which sounds when the waters start galloping up over the rocks. The

Beauport Beach

monument of two clasped hands on the headland commemorates the rescue in 1995 of the French catamaran, *Saint Malo*, which ran aground when travelling from Jersey to Sark. All 307 passengers were saved. A carved stone on the causeway recalls a story with a less happy outcome: an assistant lighthouse keeper who drowned while trying to save a tourist caught by the incoming tide.

St Ouen's Bay

This huge sandy beach is Jersey's surfing hotspot. While La Pulente at the southern end is protected from the Atlantic swell, the big rollers further north provide championship conditions. Surf schools dotted along the bay hire out equipment for windsurfing,

Corbière Lighthouse

bodyboarding and skimboarding as well as surfing. Inexperienced surfers should always keep between the red and yellow flags, where lifeguards patrol. Cafés provide sea-view terraces where you can sit and watch the pros at play over hearty breakfasts, lunches or sunset suppers. Cycle routes 1 and 3 will both take you to St Ouen's Bay.

The observation tower

On a rocky islet at the southern end of the bay, **La Rocco Tower** ⓰ was one of nine round towers that were constructed along the bay during the Napoleonic Wars. The tower took a battering during the Occupation in World War II when the Germans used it as target practice, but it has since undergone restoration. The concrete wall backing the entire bay was built by slave labourers of the Todt Organisation against tanks coming ashore from Allied landing craft. Today the west-facing wall is a useful barrier during spring tides, and provides a warm, wind-free screen for sunbathers. The spacious sands here are favourite spots among islanders for post-surf barbecues, ideally as the sun is setting. Another of the round towers still standing is the squat **Kempt Tower** ⓱ (1834) further north, one of the few surviving examples of a Martello tower.

At the southern end of the bay **Les Blanches Banques** sand dunes, where the marram grass is abundant, are a true haven for naturalists. Making their homes here are rare and aptly-named invertebrates such as the large Jersey green lizard, the blue winged grasshopper, and bloody-nosed beetle, whose name comes from the fact that when threatened, it secretes foul red liquid from its mouth which looks alarmingly similar to a drop of blood. More than 400 plant species have been recorded, no fewer than 16 of them featuring in the British red data book of endangered species.

In 1914 Jersey was called on to build a prisoner-of-war camp to accommodate 1,000 German prisoners. This was built on the lower dune plain, and by 1917 had expanded to take in 1,500 prisoners. The camp was closed in 1919.

Further north **Le Noir Pré** meadows, accessed from the Chemin de L'Ouzière, are one of the last strongholds of the loose-flowered or Jersey orchid (*Orchis laxiflora*). Guernsey is the only other place in the British Isles where the orchid can be found. In May to mid-June the meadows are a riot of colour from these and other flowering orchids. The reed beds and marshy surrounds of the nearby St Ouen's Pond (La Mare au Seigneur) draw scores of migratory birds, including sedge warblers and bearded reedlings. Marsh harriers can often be seen drifting over the reed beds.

NOTES

Set on the cliff top overlooking Corbière Lighthouse, the massive concrete observation tower was built during the German Occupation in World War II. Restored in Modernist Bauhaus style, the six-floor tower, with terrific 360 degree views from the panoramic windows of the lounge/diner, is now rented out by Jersey Heritage as stylish self-catering accommodation.

Channel Islands Military Museum

The Grande Route des Mielles (otherwise known as Five Mile Road, even though in reality it is only a little over three miles long) runs along Jersey's west coast from Les Laveurs to the St Peter/St Brelade boundary. It leads north to a clutch of visitor attractions. Above the beach a World War II German bunker is home

Catch of the day at Faulkner Fisheries

to the **Channel Islands Military Museum** ⓲ (www.jersey.com/things-to-do/attractions/listings/channel-island-military-museum; charge), devoted to German Occupation memorabilia. Exhibits include arms and ammunition, Luftwaffe brass band instruments, tins of dried eggs from Red Cross food parcels and a stark notice of the death sentence for a Jersey resident, for releasing a pigeon with a message for England.

Across the main road buses disgorge visitors at **Jersey Pearl** (www.jerseypearl.com), where you can learn all about pearls, watch the craftsmen and tour the plush showroom.

L'Etacq

The B35 then heads inland, and the road drops down to Le Grand Etacquerel, a vast expanse of reefs, better suited to rock pool

Kempt Tower

exploration than swimming. A forest close to L'Etacq was submerged when the sea level rose after the Ice Age, and on rare occasions, when the sands have been washed away by storms, you can see the remains of ancient tree stumps. The main attraction is the **Faulkner Fisheries**, (www.faulknerfisheries.com), at the far end of the bay which sell ready-cooked lobster, crabs and fresh fish from an ex-German bunker. You can also enjoy fresh and affordable barbecued seafood at their wooden benches overlooking the coast. The bunker overlooks **Le Pulec Bay**, known familiarly as Stinky Bay for reasons that will soon become apparent. The odorous seaweed is still used to fertilise some of the Jersey Royal potatoes grown on the steeply sloping hillsides (*côtils*) on the landward side.

The windswept clifftops between L'Etacq and Grosnez provide some spectacular views along the coastline. The main road diverts inland after L'Etacq but you can pick up a footpath to the top of the cliffs. Wartime relics include restored gun emplacements and bunkers from the **Moltke Battery**, which once sprawled across the headland here. (Open some Sundays; for information visit www.cios.org.je). Perched right above the sea on rapidly eroding cliffs is **Le Pinacle** ⓳, a 200ft (60m) high menhir-like stack, used as an ancient ceremonial site from the Neolithic to Roman eras. Brooding on the clifftops to the north is the **MP3 direction and range-finding tower**, another potent symbol of the German Occupation. Inland the extensive windswept heath, known as **Les Landes**, is home to Jersey's racecourse, a rifle range and an airfield for model aircraft.

Grosnez Castle

On the northwest tip of the island, the ruins of **Grosnez Castle** ⓴ stand evocatively on the heather- and gorse-clad clifftops. This

STOCKING UP ON SEAWEED

If you happen to be on the beach in autumn or winter you may see tractors loading up with vraic (pronounced 'rack') from the beach. This is the seaweed which for centuries has been used to fertilise farms bordering the coast. There are two types of vraic: the weed washed up on the beach after stormy weather, and the type cut from the rocks, which was used as fuel by fishermen who could not afford coal or wool. Vraic collection days were party-like, with whole families gathering on the beaches, men wading out to the rocks on foot or going by boat, while women and children collected ormers, crabs and limpets in profusion. Spirits were kept high with vraic buns and cider, and at the end of the day the seaweed was brought up from the bay by horse and cart, and families returned home to feast on shellfish. Cutting of vraic from the rocks was only allowed at certain times of year, and was closely supervised by parish officials. Today there are no restrictions on the public removing seaweed and it is permitted to take a vehicle on to the beach for this purpose.

Grosnez Castle

was a 14th-century fortification believed to have been destroyed by the French in the same century. On a clear day you can spot all the other Channel Islands from the castle ruins. Going from left to right these are Guernsey, Jethou, Herm and Sark, with Alderney in the far distance and the coast of Normandy to the east. At low tide you can see an extensive reef, known as the Paternoster, offshore to the east. Local legend relates that in the 16th century a boatload of women and children, who were en route to colonise Sark, were shipwrecked on the treacherous rocks here. Superstitious sailors would recite the Lord's Prayer when rounding the reef, hence the name.

The North Coast

Highlights

- **Plémont**, see page 73
- **Grève de Lecq**, see page 74
- **La Mare Wine Estate**, see page 75
- **Devil's Hole**, see page 76
- **Bonne Nuit**, see page 76
- **Bouley Bay**, see page 78
- **Rozel**, see page 79

The wild and rugged north coast, where cliffs tower above tiny sheltered harbours, couldn't be more of a contrast to the flat beaches and calm seas of the south. The peaceful north coast footpath (see page 108), stretching all the way from Grosnez in the west to Rozel in the east, is the most exhilarating walk on the island, affording spectacular sea views. The paths, flanked by wild flowers, dip down to little bays, where you can take a break at harbour-side cafés or cool off in clear waters.

Plémont

The most westerly beach is **Plémont Bay** ㉑ or, more correctly, La Grève au Lançon (Sand Eel Beach). At high tide the beach is non-existent, but twice a day the waters recede to reveal an unspoilt expanse of golden sands. This is by far the best beach on the north coast, and the longish flight of steps down and the lack of facilities keep away the crowds. The seas can get rough here, and it's popular with surfers, but normally in summer it's safe enough for bathing, and lifeguards patrol the beach for most of the day.

Behind the beach the sea has eroded the cliffs; there are caves to explore and rock pools for paddling. The family-run **Plémont Beach Café** at the top of the steps is an excellent spot for a bite, using prime Jersey produce. Parking just above the bay, where cars are lined up on the steep and narrow road, is best avoided in season. It's easier to leave your car near the bus stop at the top and take the scenic cliff path down to the beach, enjoying the views as you go.

For years the headland above the bay was the site of a derelict Pontins Holiday Camp, which was then purchased by a commercial company who wanted to build a large development. Jersey residents heaved a sigh of relief when the National Trust successfully campaigned against the project and the land was sold to the Trust. The old holiday camp was demolished and the beautiful headland restored to its natural state.

Grève de Lecq

Going eastwards Grève de Lecq (well signed off the B55, or take cycle route 1 or 4a) is the most popular of the north coast bays, with a large car park to accommodate island tour buses, a sandy beach, fishing pier and choice of eateries. Up from the bay the **Grève de Lecq Barracks** ㉒ (closed to the public) were built in 1810–15 in preparation for an expected Napoleonic invasion. British troops were garrisoned here until the 1920s. The only surviving barracks on the island, they have been restored by Jersey's National Trust, and the old officers' quarters have been turned into self-catering accommodation for tourists.

In a valley up the road the **Moulin de Lecq** (https://moulindelecq.co.uk) is the place for a pint (see page 121), either in the garden or in the olde-worlde bar where the huge cog of this former water mill provides an unusual backdrop. The great water wheel outside still functions, though it is no longer used to grind flour. During the German Occupation the water wheel was used to

PUFFINS AT PLÉMONT

The burrows in the cliffs at Plémont have been the nesting site of a small colony of puffins for many years. A century ago, there were around 200 breeding pairs on the island. By 2022 that number had dropped to just four. Climate change and food shortages, particularly the declining number of sand eels, are thought to be the causes. You will only be able to spot the puffins if you come in spring when they are nesting, but it's important to only observe them from the path, and avoid disturbing them. Better still, join one of the birding tours with local experts Neil and Alli Singleton of Birding Tours Jersey (www.jersey.com/things-to-do/events/listings/puffins-at-plemont). You'll have little trouble spotting the pair of giant, 4m-high puffins unveiled here in 2022, however. The sculpture is made of steel and willow, and was designed to highlight the precarious status of these iconic birds on the island.

power energy for searchlights to defend the bay.

The promontory east of the bay, known as **Le Câtel de Lecq**, was an Iron Age earthwork fortification, where Gallic and Roman coins were discovered. Beyond, a remote and extremely pretty beach, **Le Val Rouget**, can be accessed via a cliff path and a long dark tunnel, which you can only pass through at very low tide. The route goes via **Venus' Pool**, where you can jump from a high rock into the deep, dark waters. Youngsters love the adventure but check with locals about the tides and the route before setting off.

Gate detail at La Mare Wine Estate

La Mare Wine Estate

From Grève de Lecq the B40 takes you to the village of St Mary; from here follow signs for the Devil's Hole to reach **La Mare Wine Estate** 23 (www.lamarewineestate.com; charge). Established in 1972 on a farm dating back to the 17th century, this is Jersey's only working vineyard. From a small family-run tourist attraction, it has expanded into a professionally managed 25-acre (10-hectare) estate, producing a range of wines, ciders and spirits – along with a large selection of Jersey culinary specialities. Twenty thousand bottles are produced annually, including a red (made from a blend of Pinot Noir, Regent, and Rondo grapes), a white (a blend of Orion and Seyval Blanc), a rosé and a sparkling wine. The cider is made from a blend of the estate's own organic apples and apples from local growers, while some of the estate's apples are double distilled in a Cognac brandy pot and aged in oak casks to become Jersey apple brandy. The also produce several gins. The function room was beautifully renovated in 2019, and in 2023 the estate planted new vineyards. You can book a guided tour and tasting, or afternoon tea in the vineyard. The vineyard shop stocks black butter (see page 115). preserves and luxury chocolates as well as wines; a café with a gorgeous terrace that overlooks the vineyard is open for good coffee, delicious cream teas and simple but very tasty lunches.

Devil's Hole

From the Priory Inn car park just north of La Mare, a footpath leads down to the cliffs and Le Creux de Vis (Screw Hole) or, as it's more familiarly known, **Devil's Hole ㉔**. From a narrow causeway you can watch the waves crash dramatically into a yawning chasm in the cliff as the tides come up. This blowhole was created by the sea eroding the roof of what was once a cave. The dramatic name of Devil's Hole was acquired in the 19th century and is believed to have originated from the shipwreck of a French boat in 1851. The figurehead of the vessel was discovered in the hole here, and a local sculptor transformed it into a wooden devil with horns. A replica of the original towers over the pond beside the path that winds down to the Devil's Hole.

Bonne Nuit

Sheltering below the heather-clad cliffs, the next bay is picturesque **Bonne Nuit ㉕** (Good Night). The name was recorded back in the 12th century, refuting the long-held belief that it derived from King Charles II's parting words *Bonne nuit, belle Jersey*, when he left from the port here after his exile on the island. The name probably referred to the shelter that the little harbour offered to sailors overnight.

The unspoilt bay comprises little more than a stone jetty sheltering the harbour; a sand, shingle and rock beach taken up by little fishing boats that go out daily for lobsters and crabs; and the popular **Bonne Nuit Beach Café** (https://bonnenuitbeachcafe.co.uk) with lovely views of the bay. A familiar sight at low or mid tide is the gaggle of ducks waddling across the beach, hopeful of a crumb from the cream teas served up by the café.

On the rugged headland east of the bay the British-built **La Crête Fort** (1830) used to be a weekend retreat for the island's lieutenant-governor. Now anyone can holiday here through Jersey Heritage (www.jerseyheritage.org). There are a couple of simply-furnished bedrooms, wonderful views over open seas to Guernsey,

Colourful cottages at Rozel

Sark and the coast of France, and a secluded walled garden where you can sit and contemplate the sunset.

Bouley Bay

Two other historic forts, built in the line of defence against the French, have been converted for holiday lets at **Bouley Bay** ㉖ to the southeast. Fort Leicester (named after Queen Elizabeth I's Earl of Leicester) sleeps up to eight. The more basic L'Etacquerel Fort (www.jerseyheritage.org/stay/heritage-lets/letacquerel-fort) has 'stone hut' accommodation for 30 people – and space for up to 60 by day. Accessed via a steep coastal path, and a high wooden bridge over the moat, this is a peaceful atmospheric spot for a back-to-basics gathering. There are no utilities (prepare yourselves for composting toilets only) and you will need to bring your own sleeping bags.

Bouley Bay consists of no more than a steeply shelving pebble-and-rock beach (voted one of the cleanest in the UK), the Water's Edge Apartments and a diving school. With its deep, clear and pond-like waters, this is the main place on Jersey for scuba diving. It's also a good spot for kayaking, swimming and snorkelling – or just sitting at **Mad Mary's Café** (www.jersey.com/things-to-do/food-and-drink/listings/mad-marys-beach-cafe) right on the beach and enjoying the views. Bouley Bay is the venue for the British Hill Climb Championships, and three times a year the peace

NOTES

Jersey abounds with myth and superstition. On the north coast tales used to spread of the Black Dog of Bouley Bay, a terrifying beast with huge teeth and eyes the size of saucers that roamed the coastline. The tales were probably invented by smugglers hoping to scare away parishioners from the coast while they landed their cargoes of brandy and tobacco.

Rozel harbour

of the bay is shattered as saloon cars, racing cars, sports cars and motor bikes tear up the steep hill.

Rozel

Nestling below wooded slopes, **Rozel** 27 is a romantic little creek, with a handful of fishermen's cottages, a small port and shingle beach. There has always been a fishing harbour here, and in the 1820s it was the base for around 30 oyster-fishing boats. Today fishermen go out for lobster and crab the Hungry Man kiosk by the pier serves a great crab sandwich which you can wash down with a mug of tea (https://thehungryman.je). Behind the bay barracks were built in 1810 but the anticipated attack on Rozel never took place – despite it being the closest point on the island to France. The barracks have been converted into a luxury private home.

Behind the bay the **Vallée de Rozel** is lush and verdant, planted with subtropical trees and shrubs. Tucked away in the valley is the elegant **Château La Chaire Hotel** (https://chateau-la-chaire.co.uk) with over 8 acres (3 hectares) of beautiful gardens and grounds, created by Samuel Curtis, a 19th-century botanist and former director of Kew Gardens. Curtis first saw the site in 1841 and, having searched all over the British Isles, instantly knew that this steep-sided valley, with a stream running onto the shingle beach of Rozel Bay, was the ideal spot for his subtropical plant paradise. He built a small house here under the cliffs and created a series of paths and terraces. The house was pulled down at the end of the century, and a grander one took its place (now the hotel). During

L'Etacquerel Fort at sunset

the Occupation the Germans dug up some of the prized trees, and today few of Curtis' original species survive.

Jersey Zoo

'The world is as delicate and as complicated as a spider's web. If you touch one thread you send shudders running through all the other threads. We are not just touching the webs, we are tearing great holes in it...' *Gerald Durrell* (author and naturalist).

Gerald Durrell's first intelligible word is said to have been 'zoo'. From the age of six he had wanted to create a safe place for his collection of animals. In 1959, 34 years later, he realised his childhood dream by creating Jersey Zoo. It was set up not as a zoo in the conventional sense but as a sanctuary and breeding centre for some of the world's most endangered animal species. Durrell's objectives were to provide a safe haven for these rare species, build up colonies, then send them to organisations worldwide, who would return them to the wild and reintroduce them to areas where they had become extinct.

Durrell chose the dodo as symbol of the zoo, thereby demonstrating his commitment to saving rare species from the fate that befell the flightless bird from Mauritius. The zoo is operated by the **Durrell Wildlife Conservation Trust** ㉘ (www.durrell.org; charge; bus Nos 3, 13 and 23; cycle routes 1 and 3a). Since 1977 conservationists from around the world have been trained in the theory and practice of endangered species recovery, and the trust has earned a worldwide reputation for pioneering conservation techniques. Durrell died in 1995 and is survived by his widow, zoologist and author Dr Lee McGeorge Durrell, who continues his dedicated work at the trust.

Conservation mainly focuses on the island areas of the Galápagos, the Caribbean islands, Madagascar and Indian Ocean islands and India – but not forgetting Jersey's own dwindling amphibians such as the agile frog and the common toad (or *crapaud*), the island's beloved mascot. Among the species that have been pulled back from the brink are the pink pigeons and kestrels from Mauritius, the St Lucia whiptail, the thick-billed parrots from Arizona, and the pygmy hog, the world's oldest and rarest pig, which has been successfully reintroduced to the wildlife sanctuary in Assam, northeast India. In the late 1980s a couple of St Lucia parrots flew back to the Caribbean with British Airways, accompanied by the prime minister of St Lucia who had come to Jersey specifically to escort them home. Recent projects include the Jamaican boa or yellowsnake, the Madagascan teal and flat-tailed tortoise, the Floreana mocking bird from the Galápagos and the Montserrat mountain chicken, which is in fact a large frog, tasting of chicken. The latter is endangered by a deadly fungal disease discovered on the Caribbean island.

Bronze statue of zoologist and author Gerald Durrell

If you're expecting unhappy animals cramped in cages you're in for a pleasant surprise. The setting is a 32-acre (13 hectare) oasis of woodland, landscaped lawns and water gardens, surrounding an 18th-century granite manor house. Wherever possible the trust has tried to cultivate the native habitat for family groups of the endangered species. Certainly by average zoo standards, the animals

GERALD DURRELL

Gerald Durrell was born in India and from an early age collected 'everything from minnows to woodlice'. After the death of his father, when Gerald was only 3 years old, his mother brought him and his sister to England to be educated. Durrell detested school, left at the age of 9, and was educated by private tutors who concentrated on what he loved: natural history. Four idyllic years from the age of 10 were spent in Corfu, surrounded by a menagerie of animals. This led to his best-known novel, *My Family and Other Animals* (1956), which has sold five million copies. The hit TV series, The Durrells (2016–2019) was based on Durrell's three autobiographical books about his early years living in Corfu. At the age of 21 he inherited £3,000, which funded his first animal-collecting expedition – to the British Cameroons – and he spent the next decade collecting animals for British zoos. Durrell wrote 33 books, hosted TV series and radio programmes and won nine international awards for leadership in conservation.

do look remarkably content. The golden-headed lion tamarins roam in the woods, the gorillas play in a spacious compound, flamingos wade in the lake, reptiles have their own tropical habitat-simulated quarters, aye-ayes have a special nocturnal unit, and orangutans swing from ropes or stick twigs in logs to prise out the honey.

Among the favourite residents are the western lowland gorillas, led by the silverback male Badongo. One of the zoo's most famous residents was Jambo, the 'gentle giant' western lowland gorilla who hit the headlines in 1986 when he protected a 5-year-old boy who fell into the compound. Jambo, who died in 1992, was the first male gorilla to be reared in captivity. Hlala Kahilli, one of the current gorillas at the zoo, is descended from him. The gorilla house was completely rebuilt in 2025.

There are many ways visitors can become more involved in the zoo, from adopting an animal to volunteering – and the wildlife camp here with its glamping tents is a fantastic place to stay.

Flamingos at Jersey Zoo

The East Coast

Highlights

- **St Catherine's Breakwater**, see page 85
- **Geoffrey's Leap**, see page 87
- **Mont Orgueil Castle**, see page 88
- **Gorey**, see page 90
- **The Royal Bay of Grouville**, see page 91
- **Seymour Tower**, see page 92

Star attractions of the east coast are Mont Orgueil Castle (www.jerseyheritage.org/visit/places-to-visit/mont-orgueil-castle; charge), a majestic fortress that played a pivotal role in the island's history, and the picturesque port of Gorey, which shelters beneath its walls. From here the Royal Bay of Grouville, sheltered from westerly winds, stretches southwards for nearly 2 miles (3km). Queen Victoria was so impressed by the spacious, sandy bay that she added the royal prefix after her visit in 1859.

St Catherine's Breakwater

The most significant feature of **St Catherine's Bay** is the massive **breakwater** ㉙ which encloses it on the northern side. In response to coastal installations, which the French had created at Cherbourg, the British decided to build a naval base with a large deepwater harbour at St Catherine's. Warnings that the waters were too shallow for warships went unheeded and in 1847 breakwaters were built both here and at Archirondel Tower to the south. By the time the St Catherine's breakwater was complete, eight years on, the British realised their blunder and the project was abandoned. Today the breakwater provides a bracing half-mile (0.8km) walk, a shelter for dinghies and a useful pier for anglers. From the lighthouse at the end there are fine views of the coast to the south, the small pebble and rock bay of Fliquet to the north, which you can reach on foot, and the rocky islets known as

One of Jersey Zoo's western lowland gorillas

Anne Port, in the south of St Catherine's Bay

Les Écréhous (see box). On a clear day you can see as far as the Normandy coast.

Just south of the breakwater there's a **German bunker** and tunnel complex which can be visited (www.stcatherinesbunker.com; charge). Until 2023, the bunker was used to house tanks of around 6,500 turbot, which were sold to restaurateurs, fishmongers and the public.

From St Catherine's Bay you can walk all the way to Gorey – or drive on the coastal B29. A distinctive landmark is the red and white **Archirondel Tower** ⓿ on the eponymous beach, built in 1792 as a garrison for artillery soldiers. The tower has been restored and is now available for 'stone hut' holiday accommodation. Inland, a walk through **St Catherine's Wood** provides a delightful shady diversion from the coast.

Geoffrey's Leap

The rocky promontory between Anne Port Bay and Gorey Harbour is known as Le Saut Geoffroi or **Geoffrey's Leap**, after a popular Jersey legend. A renowned womaniser, Geoffrey was convicted of sexual harassment and sentenced to be thrown off the cliffs here on to the rocks below. Miraculously he missed the rocks and surfaced at Anne Port to the north. The reaction among islanders was divided: some wanted him thrown off the cliffs again, others, including some female admirers, saw his survival as proof of innocence. Seeing another opportunity to impress local women, Geoffrey took it upon himself to repeat the leap – but this time dashed his brains out.

Off a country lane inland from Geoffrey's Leap and approached along a leafy path is **La Pouquelaye de Faldouet** ㉛ (www.jerseyheritage.org/visit/places-to-visit/faldouet-dolmen; free) an impressive and somewhat elusive 50ft (15m) long neolithic passage grave. Dolmens like these played an important role in the

KINGS OF LES ÉCRÉHOUS

The reef of rocks lying mid-way between Jersey and Normandy, known as Les Écréhous, has been part of Jersey's bailiwick since 1953. The reef expands by about 80 percent at low tide and it's a lovely spot to visit on a boat trip in season. A couple of 'kings' have inhabited the reef: in 1848 Phillipe Pinel lived with his wife on Blanche Île for 46 years and was proclaimed 'king' by local fishermen who lived in the huts here. In the 1960s Alphonse Le Gastelois, an eccentric fisherman and farmhand who was suspected of being the mystery child attacker known as 'the beast of Jersey', moved to Les Écréhous and lived alone here for 14 years, claiming that the island belonged to him. (By the time he returned to Jersey, the real beast, one Edward Paisnel, had been tracked down, convicted of 13 counts of assault, rape and sodomy and sentenced to 30 years' imprisonment).

rich folklore of the island, and this one, tucked away off a rural lane, retains an air of mysterious antiquity. Look on any Jersey 10p coin and you will see a picture of it.

Mont Orgueil Castle

Even if you have never visited **Mont Orgueil Castle** 32 (www.jersey heritage.org/visit/places-to-visit/mont-orgueil-castle; charge), it is likely to look familiar – the photogenic fortress is reproduced on countless postcards, holiday brochures and guides. Commanding a spectacular promontory above the harbour, built into the granite rocks, it makes a wonderful backdrop to Gorey Harbour, both by day and by night when the battlements are floodlit.

La Pouquelaye de Faldouet

The earliest fortifications date back to the very early 13th century when King John had lost control of Normandy and the island needed protection against the threat of French invasion. Built in a concentric series of defences, the castle proved to be an impregnable fortress. As warfare changed the fortification was expanded and strengthened. Fifteen French attacks were made between 1204 and 1600, most of them unsuccessful. One notable exception was the French invasion of 1468 which resulted in a seven-year occupation.

Mont Orgueil Castle

Mont Orgueil was essentially a bow-and-arrow castle and by the late 16th century it was no longer able to sustain modern warfare. Elizabeth Castle, equipped with cannons, was built on Jersey's south coast. Mont Orgueil would have been razed to the ground were it not for the intervention of Sir Walter Raleigh, then governor of the island, who decided that the stately fort should stay. It became a prison in the 17th century, then in 1789 a refuge for aristocrats fleeing the reign of terror and the guillotine in France. In 1907 the castle was finally given by the Crown to the States of Jersey and in 1996 Queen Elizabeth II handed it over to the islanders.

A network of ancient, dark staircases and cobbled passageways lead up to lofty ramparts. At the top Somerset Tower, adapted under the German Occupation as an observation post, commands magnificent 360-degree views of the island and across to France. Within the castle there is plenty to explore in the way of medieval keeps, cellars, towers, chapels and gun platforms. History is kept alive with audio-visual presentations, large artworks (such as the gruesome carving showing the fate that might await those defending the castle from attack), twice-weekly hawking demonstrations and occasional tales and displays of Tudor life. The castle also makes a perfect backdrop for occasional medieval drama and re-enactments.

Gorey

Below the castle walls **Gorey Harbour** is a picture postcard ensemble of quaint houses, pubs and seafood cafés, clustering around a

Gorey Harbour

harbour of fishing boats, yachts and pleasure craft. In the early 19th century the port grew prosperous on the oyster trade, becoming known as 'the pearl of the east'. The British muscled in on the lucrative industry and by the 1830s there were around 260 oyster vessels and 1,400 fishermen – along with 600–700 women and children who gave a helping hand. Fishing cottages were built at Gorey and a pier to protect the oyster fleet, but the fishermen became over-ambitious and by the 1860s the oyster beds were almost exhausted. The village returned to its shellfish-producing traditions by introducing oyster and mussel farms in the last century. Up to 600 tonnes of oysters are now produced annually – and not surprisingly, they feature on virtually every Gorey menu. At very low tide you can see the oyster beds in Grouville Bay, and, more prominent, the rows of wooden poles where the Bouchot mussels grow.

The Royal Bay of Grouville

The huge expanse of sands stretching south from Gorey Harbour, known as the **Royal Bay of Grouville** ㉝, attracts water sports aficionados, joggers, sunbathers and swimmers. Bathing is safe but with the huge tidal movement you should be prepared for quite a walk out to sea. In July and August, Gorey Watersports organises kayaking, water-skiing, wakeboarding, speedboat trips and banana rides – wetsuits, life-jackets and tuition are all provided.

During World War II the Germans used a million tonnes of Grouville sand to construct the concrete fortifications around the coast. The spacious Grouville Common that borders the beach saw duels fought in the 18th century, and horse racing in Victorian times. If you're strolling on the common watch out for stray golf balls. This is home to the exclusive Royal Jersey Golf Club, where Grouville-born Harry Vardon (six times British Open Championship winner) trained in the early years. Vardon was the first professional golfer to play in knickerbockers and is famous for the overlapping grip which bears his name and which is used

La Rocque Harbor

by the vast majority of golfers. The club has been here since 1878 and remained unchanged until the German Occupation when the links were transformed into a minefield. Today the club is the most exclusive on the island. Visitors are welcome provided they are members of a recognised golf club.

This whole stretch of coast, from St Helier Harbour to Gorey Pier, is a protected site, characterised by weather-worn reefs, mud, sand and shingle shores and exposed twice a day by one of the largest tidal ranges in the world.

Seymour Tower

The predominantly rocky shoreline to the south of Grouville Bay is guarded by a series of towers, built in the 18th century but never actually used to defend the island. Some of the towers have been turned into private residences. At the southeastern tip **La Rocque Harbour** was the arrival point of Baron de Rullecourt and his troops, who made a surprise night-time landing in 1781, only to be defeated in the Battle of Jersey. At low tide you can walk out to Seymour Tower, isolated on a rocky islet 2 miles (3km) off La Rocque Point. The walk takes you over an eerie wilderness of gullies, sandbars, reefs and rocks and the low-lying coast provides a rich breeding ground for thousands of wintering waders, gulls and wildfowl. Watch out for the tides – the sea comes galloping in at a frighteningly fast rate.

Those with a sense of adventure might like to stay overnight in **Seymour Tower** 34 (www.jerseyheritage.org/stay/heritage-lets/seymour-tower), which can accommodate up to seven guests, sleeping in bunk beds. There are no luxuries like running water but drinking water is provided, as are logs for the wood-burning stove. You carry your own food, clothes and sleeping bags, and carry back all waste (including bagged toilet waste) which will need to be disposed of onshore. The only hitch, at least for independently minded visitors, is that you must be accompanied by a Seymour Tower Guide who guides you to and from the tower and stays the night (www.jerseyheritage.org).

The Seymour Tower at low tide

Jersey is a water sports paradise

Things to do

Culture

Jersey Museum, Art Gallery and Victorian House (www.jerseyheritage.org/visit/places-to-visit/jersey-museum) in St Helier is Jersey's premier art gallery, where you can learn about the island's history and heritage, admire masterpieces like A Jersey Lily by Sir John Everett Millais, and there's a new display centring on the island's bid to become a UNESCO World Geopark.

The Maritime Museum (www.jerseyheritage.org/visit/places-to-visit/maritime-museum-occupation-tapestry), also in St Helier, is the island's other big-hitter when it comes to museums and galleries, and tells the story of how the island's history and landscape have been shaped by the sea. The museum is also home to the Occupation Tapestries Gallery.

The Harbour Gallery (St Helier; https://theharbourgalleryjersey.com) is the largest working and exhibiting art and craft gallery in the Channel Islands.

Art House Jersey (www.arthousejersey.je) is a charity supporting artists in Jersey; it hosts temporary exhibitions by contemporary local artists. There are also numerous small arts and crafts centres and galleries scattered across the island, where you can see the works of local artists, potters, glassblowers and the like. **The Jersey Arts Centre** (St Helier; www.artscentre.je) is a non-profit-making organisation that stages contemporary and classical concerts plus theatre and art exhibitions.

The **Jersey Opera House** (St Helier; www.jerseyoperahouse.co.uk) has been beautifully restored and stages concerts, drama, dance and very occasionally, operas. **Fort Regent** (www.gov.je/events) hosts occasional classical and popular concerts, exhibitions and fairs. The spring and summer months see several large music festivals on Jersey, including the Weekender Festival (https://weekender.je). The National Trust for Jersey stages summer

Heading out into the surf at St Ouen's Bay

concerts at Mont Grantez, and there are theatre productions in the grounds of Samarares Manor.

Ballet d'Jèrri (www.ballet.je) is a world-class dance company based in Jersey, founded in 2022 and quickly establishing itself as Jersey's National Ballet. Ballet d'Jèrri develops new works in collaboration with leading international choreographers, which are premiered in Jersey before touring overseas.

Outdoor Activities

Despite its diminutive size, Jersey has boundless of scope for outdoor adventure, from hiking and kayaking to surfing and scuba diving. The one constant through all of these is the sea, and Jersey's beautiful coastline – from big surfing beaches to rock-bound coves, clear diving waters and gently shelving sands. So whether you fancy hiking a clifftop trail with views stretching out across the La Manche, or are in the mood for enjoying the vast sweep of sandy beach that is St Ouen's Bay, Jersey won't disappoint.

Swimming. The water is not as warm as the Mediterranean – sea temperatures average around 17°C (63°F) in summer – but Jersey is idyllic for swimming. Once past the paddlers, you can have huge expanses of clear seawater all to yourself. Beware, however, of heavy swells and swimming on outgoing tides. Lifeguards patrol St Ouen's beach, St Brelade's Bay, Plémont and some of the other main beaches from mid-May to the end of September. The patrolled areas are indicated by red and yellow flags. Red flags indicate that sea conditions are dangerous.

Surfing. With towering Atlantic rollers and a huge beach, St Ouen's bay on the west coast, is *the* place to surf. The Jersey Surfboard Club is one of the oldest in Europe, established back in 1959. Surf schools can arrange equipment hire and give you advice on how to ride the rollers. Jersey Surf School (www.jerseysurfschool.co.uk) at the Watersplash offers professional surf coaching by accredited instructors and a full range of equipment for hire. Unless you're a real pro, keep to the areas between the yellow and red flags, which are surveyed by lifeguards. Bodyboarding and windsurfing equipment are also available, though beginner windsurfers are better off at St Brelade's, St Aubin's or Grouville where the waters are calmer.

Kitesurfing, Wakeboarding and Water-skiing. Wakeboarding is available at St Brelade's Bay, St Aubin's Bay and the Royal Bay of Grouville. The best spots for water-skiing are St Aubin's Bay and Grouville, where the waters are not too choppy. St Ouen's Bay is the spot for kitesurfing, depending on which way the wind's blowing.

Blokarting. Race along the sands of St Ouen's Bay – adrenalin-specialists Absolute Adventures (www.absoluteadventures.je) offer blokarting at Le Braye.

Kayaking. Jersey's clear waters, remote coves and rich marine life make for excellent kayaking. Kayaks can be hired at the main

Playing at the Royal Jersey Golf Club, Grouville

beaches. The kayak specialists are Jersey Kayak Adventures (www.jersey kayakadventures.co.uk) who operate from venues all over the island. Tours are suitable for all ages and abilities, and all equipment is provided.

SUPing. There are several places where you can rent standup paddle boards on the island, including Jono's Watersports in St Brelade's Bay (https://jonoswater sports.com) and the Bouley Bay Dive Centre (https://scubadivingjersey.com). Absolute Adventures (www.absoluteadventures.je) in St Brelade's Bay offer SUP tours.

Sailing. Marinas and harbours have excellent facilities for sailors but beginners should beware of sunken reefs, big tides and strong currents. Experienced sailors can charter boats or join local regattas. Flexible day or evening sailing trips, focusing on the waters around Jersey, are organised by **Jersey Yachting** (www.jersey yachting.co.uk), who sail from St Helier.

Diving. Bouley Bay, with its clear, calm waters, is the most popular part of the island for scuba diving. The longstanding Bouley Bay Dive Centre (www.scubadivingjersey.com), welcomes beginners and experts alike. Divers with experience can dive down to wrecks of ships sunk in World War II and other vessels that have been deliberately scuttled to provide shelter for marine life.

Hiking. Jersey packs in plenty of scope for hiking, from gentle strolls along seafront promenades, or down leafy lanes through woodland valleys, to the more dramatic north coast cliffs. In addition to the footpaths there are 50 miles (80km) of Green Lanes, with a speed limit of 15 mph (24kmph) giving priority to pedestrians, cyclists and horse riders.

The North Coast is the best place for walking. The **North Coast Footpath** runs for 15 miles (24km) from **Grosnez** to **Rozel**. Some sections are quite steep, particularly as the path climbs up from the bays, but there is nothing seriously challenging. The walk can either be done in its entirety over a very long day, or in separate, relatively short, sections at a gentler pace. The scenery is best in spring when wild flowers are in full bloom and birds come ashore to nest. The path occasionally diverts from the coast, but the route is well signed. Getting there and back is best done by bus. No. 3 goes from St Helier to Rozel, No. 8 returns from Grosnez. One of the most spectacular stretches is Bonne Nuit to Bouley Bay (4 miles/2.5km, served by No. 4 bus from St Helier). You could also walk west from Bonne Nuit to La Saline. Check the Jersey bus timetable on www.libertybus.je.

Walks in the southwest corner of the island afford some splendid coastal views. **Portelet Common** on

There are plenty of lovely walks to be had in Jersey

Jersey Opera House

the headland between Portelet Bay and Ouaisné Bay commands a stunning panorama over Ouaisné and St Brelade's Bay to the north-west, and over Portelet Bay to the east. **Noirmont Promontory** is not quite as scenic but provides pleasant clifftop strolls and historic interest in its German Occupation relics. A longer walk takes you all the way from **Ouaisné Bay** to **La Corbière**. Features such as the island prison and desalination plant don't enhance the scenery and the track occasionally diverts inland, but most of this rugged cliff path is unspoilt, with superb sea views. The walk ends with the striking view of Corbière Lighthouse. From **St Helier** to **St Aubin** the long seafront promenade makes an ideal leisurely stroll or cycle ride; from St Aubin you can continue to Corbière along the old railway route, now a peaceful cycle- and footpath through varied scenery, from red squirrel-inhabited woodland to gorse-clad heathland. It's a gentle climb of 4 miles (6.4km), and you can return to St Aubin or St Helier by bus No.12a.

Cycling. No distance is too far to cycle – though the hills can be strenuous (not a problem if you hire ebikes) and on occasions the local 4x4s leave you little space on the narrow country lanes. Cyclists should plan their routes around the 60-mile (96km) signposted cycle network, including 50 miles (80km) of Green Lanes, which carry a 15mph (24kmph) speed limit for cars (usually, but not always, adhered to). Jersey Tourism provides a free map detailing cycling routes and the website gives details for self-guided bike tours. One of the easiest and most attractive routes, suitable for families with small children, is the designated footpath/cycle ride following the old railway line from St Aubin to Corbière. Check

WALKING TOURS

Escorted walks take place almost every day from April to September and themes cover all aspects of the island, including wildlife, local customs, maritime history, smuggling and the German Occupation. Tours are led by enthusiastic and knowledgeable guides and the fees are very affordable. More expensive, but well worth it, are the occasional 'Moonwalks', at low tide only, across the lunar-like landscape to Seymour Tower or Icho Tower on the southeast coast. The tides can be treacherous here, and going alone is not advised. You can also visit the oyster and mussel beds off La Rocque Harbour, learn about their cultivation then sample oysters at the local pub. The Jersey Tourism website (www.jersey.com/walking-in-jersey) has details of self-guided walks, with information on length and time, degree of difficulty, transport, attractions en route and refreshment stops. Their free walking guide can be picked up at the tourist office or downloaded from the website. Jersey Walk Adventures (www.jerseywalkadventures.co.uk) offer guided walks with a variety of themes, among them Seaweed Foraging, Oyster Trails and Bioluminescence on the Beach (an evening walk revealing glow-in-the-dark fireflies or worms).

out the detailed cycle map on the Jersey Tourism website (www.jersey.com/holidays/active/cycling).

Bush camps. Discover wild edible and medicinal plants, cook on a beach fire, learn natural navigating skills, make cordage using plants and trees and construct your own shelter. Activities at Wild Adventures include rock climbing, coasteering, abseiling, boogie-boarding and cycle tours as well as 6-day survival courses. Accommodation is offered in yurts. For more information contact Wild Adventures (www.wildadventuresjersey.com).

Golf. Jersey has half a dozen golf courses, three of these championship level, and an impressive pedigree. Harry Vardon, six-times winner of the British Open, was born here, and Ian Woosnam is an island resident. Proof of handicap is required at two of the 18-hole championship courses, **La Moye** (La Route Orange, St Brelade; www.lamoyegolfclub.co.uk) and the **Royal Jersey Golf Club** (La Chemin au Grèves, Grouville; www.royaljersey.com), but not at the 18-hole **Les Mielles Golf & Country Club** (St Ouen's Bay; www.lesmielles.com). The 9-hole courses are Wheatlands (off Le Vieux Beaumont, St Peter; www.wheatlandsjersey.com), **Les Ormes Leisure Village** (St Brelade; www.lesormesjersey.co.uk), and **St Clements Golf and Sports Centre** (Plat Douet Road, St Clement; www.stclementsgolfandsportscentre.co.uk).

Outdoor Jersey for kids. For a traditional family holiday, Jersey all has the ideal ingredients: acres of sandy beaches, crab-filled rock pools, numerous sporting activities and a variety of family attractions. Top of the list should be **Jersey Zoo**, whose gorillas, orangutans, fruit bats and other endangered species will keep youngsters entertained (and educated) for at least half a day. The **Valley Activity Centre** at St Brelade (www.valleyadventure.je) is ideal for older children – and adults. The attractive valley here is the setting for a range of exciting activities, from zip wires, aerial trekking and Powerfan freefall (jumping from a 40ft (12m) tower), to coasteering. There's a huge **skatepark** out at St Ouen's Bay, completed in 2022 and one of

The Pallot steam museum

the largest in the British Isles (www.skateboardjersey.org).

The best beach for youngsters is **St Brelade's Bay**, with its great swathe of gently sloping sands and shallow waters, bucket-and-spade shops and child-friendly cafés. Children who are used to warm swimming pools may find the sea water on the cool side but it's never too cold for paddling or splashing around in the shallows. The neighbouring **Ouaisné Bay** has some great rock pools at the far end where children can mess around fishing for shrimps, crabs and devil fish. Older children who are strong swimmers will love bodyboarding on the windswept bay of St Ouen's – or just sitting at a beachside café watching the stand-up surfers catching the Atlantic rollers. On a rainy day take children to **Aqua Splash** (www.aquasplash.je) at St Helier's Waterfront Centre, which has an indoor pool with wave machine and bubble pool.

Cigarette packet dogs at St Aubin's Harbour Gallery

Time to unwind. If you find yourself in need of some pampering and time to unwind after exploring the island's great outdoors, Jersey has you well covered in the form of half a dozen plush spa centres. At the **Spa Sirène** in the Royal Yacht Hotel you can unwind with a steam mud *rasul*, sauna, or hydrotherapy bath, and chill out in the indoor vitality pool or under ice-cold bucket showers. Hotel de France's **Ayush Wellness Spa** is based on ancient Hindu health and healing principles, while the chic **Club Hotel & Spa** has a swish spa that offers all kinds of feel-good treatments. At the Grand Jersey Hotel's luxury **Grand Spa**, guests and residents are pampered in six treatment rooms and at St Brelade's, the spa at the **L'Horizon Hotel** overlooks the beautiful bay.

Shopping

Jersey is not a full member of the EU, and VAT is non-existent. However, this doesn't mean that the shops are packed with bargains. Many of them put up prices for 'freight surcharge', then add to this the 5 percent Goods and Services tax, and the prices are around the same as those in the UK. Moreover, not all goods are VAT free – some shops retain VAT on goods that have come from the UK. The best buys are wines, spirits and tobacco and, to a lesser extent, cosmetics, perfume and jewellery, which are all duty free.

The main shopping centre is St Helier, which has a pleasant pedestrianised High Street with the usual chain stores, plus department stores, gift shops and a large number of jewellers and shops selling cosmetics. As well as browsing here don't miss the indoor **Central Market**, a Victorian gem packed with stalls selling everything from fruit and veg to antiques and jewellery, nor the **Fish Market** to see the catch of the day for the markets). **Liberty Wharf** on the waterfront is a covered shopping mall converted from Victorian granite warehouses. It has a mix of UK chain stores and Jersey boutiques, with plenty of cafés.

Jersey Pottery (www.jerseypottery.com) is renowned for ceramics These can be bought at their shop in St Helier, along with other outlets. The pottery is now made in the UK, Europe and other countries.

The **Harbour Gallery** (https://theharbourgalleryjersey.com) which has now moved to St Helier from its original location in St Aubin, is a large, well-run arts and crafts centre, with regularly changing contemporary exhibitions and some innovative paintings, textiles, sculpture and designer fashion by over 100 local artists.

Some other popular shopping outlets are spread across the island. The best known of these is **Jersey Pearl** at St Ouen (www.jerseypearl.com) where you can have your own necklace made or choose from an extensive range of cultured, freshwater or simulated pearls. **Catherine Best** at Les Chenolles, St Peter (www.catherinebest.com), who is based in a lovely old windmill, creates innovative pieces of jewellery, often from rare, fabulously coloured gemstones. **Marc McCarty** (www.instagram.com/mccarty.marc) is the only glassblower in the Channel Islands, working from a small studio at the Devil's Hole. Also have a look at **Aida de la Herrán Jewellery** in St Savior (www.facebook.com/aidadelaherranjewellery).

For less expensive souvenirs have a browse at **Little Wren** (www.facebook.com/littlewrenjersey) in St Helier's Central Market. Another good place to shop for gifts is **Jersey Lavender** (https://

jerseylavender.co.uk) inland from St Brelade's Bay, where you can buy bath foams, shower gels, essential oils, soaps and candles, all made with the lavender grown in their fields.

The best foodie souvenir of Jersey is of course a jar of black butter, which you can pick up at **Maison de Jersey** in St Helier (www.maisondejersey.com). Although chocoholics may prefer a spree at **Chocadyllic** (www.chocadyllic.co.uk), an artisan chocolatier.

A bottle of Jersey gin certainly makes for a good souvenir – buy direct from **Sea Level Eco Distillery** (https://sealeveldistillery.co.uk), Jersey Cow (www.thejerseycowdistillery.com/home), **La Mare Wine Estate** (www.lamarewineestate.com) which also has its own apple brandy, and **La Côte Distillery** (https://lacotedistillery.com).

For other Jersey specialities look for the red logo and check out the website of Genuine Jersey (www.genuinejersey.je), which promotes local produce. This covers crafts and jewellery as well as food and drink.

Nightlife

Not surprisingly, most of Jersey's nightlife centres on St Helier. **The Drift** (https://theroyalyacht.com/bars/the-drift) housed in the Royal Yacht Club Hotel remains one of Jersey's top nightlife spots, with DJs, live music and a dance floor. For smaller cocktail venues head to **The Blind Pig** with its 1920s style decor, **The Don** (https://thedon.je), or **Melting Pot** (www.meltingpot.je) where the ambience is set firmly in the 70s. For details of concerts, live bands or DJs, pick up a copy of the *Jersey Evening Post*.

For a completely different take on Jersey nightlife – join a night-time guided tour of the lunar landscape that is the exposed seabed at low tide, wandering among rocks whose surface glows with otherworldly bioluminescence (https://jerseywalkadventures.co.uk). Or try a nocturnal guided tour of some of Jersey's war relics and bunkers (www.jersey.com/things-to-do/tours/listings/bunkers-at-night).

Fun among the rock pools at Ouaisné Bay

Festivals

Jersey has plenty on its festival calendar, from the likes of the Liberation Day celebrations and the vibrant Battle of Flowers to excellent music festivals such as Weekender.

Calendar of Events

For a full listing of festivals and events happening in Jersey, go to www.jersey.com/events or pick up a current copy of the *What's On* guide for the events of the month.

March: *Taste Jersey* (www.tastejersey.co.uk) is a celebration of the island's local culinary scene, offering various dining experiences and events.

April: *Delicious Jersey Food Festival* (https://jerseyhospitality.com/events) is the island's newest foodie festival, launched in 2025.

May: *Liberation Day* (9 May): celebrating the liberation from German Occupying forces during World War II. Towards the end of May the *Jersey Food Festival* celebrates the best from local food producers, chefs and artisans. The *Jersey Boat Show* (www.jerseyboatshow.com) is the largest free event in the Channel Islands. *Lib Jersey* (https://lib.j) is a two-day electronic music festival held on St Helier's Royal Square.
June: *National Trust for Jersey Sunset Concerts at Mont Grantez* (www.nationaltrust.je); *Early Summer Flower Show* (www.royaljersey.co.uk).
July: *Out There* (https://out-there.je) is a two-day electronic music festival, in the past held beside the Val de la Mare Reservoir, in 2025 this changed to the Royal Jersey Showground. Also in July are *Fête de St Hélier,* and *Jersey Premier Brass* summer concerts (https://jerseypremierbrass.org.je).
August: *Battle of Flowers* (www.battleofflowers.com), held from Friday to Sunday on the second weekend in August: a spectacular, carnival-like parade of flower-decked floats, musicians and entertainers. The Friday evening sees the Moonlight Parade of flower-covered floats. *Gorey Fête* in mid-August is a day of beach events, games, stalls, fairground rides and music.
September: The *Jersey International Air Display* (www.jerseyairdisplay.org.uk) is an immensely popular event that has been running annually since 1952 and is one of the biggest free airshows in the British Isles. *The Weekender Festival* (https://weekender.je) is Jersey's largest music festival, launched in 2018, and bringing a world-class lineup of musicians and street performers to the island.
October: Autumn events include the *Royal Jersey Horticultural Show's Autumn Fair* (www.royaljersey.co.uk/show) and *La Faîs'sie d'Cidre,* the lively Cider Festival at Hamptonne Country Life Museum.
October–November: Restaurants are packed out during the hugely succesful *Tennerfest,* six weeks (Oct–mid-Nov) when fixed menus start at £10 at over 100 restaurants.
December: *La Fête de Noué,* a Christmas festival, with street entertainment, parades and markets in St Helier.

Food and drink

Eating out is an important part of life on the island and Jersey residents, and its visitors, are spoilt for choice. A vast array of fabulously fresh seafood is caught around the island's shores, delicious Jersey Royal potatoes are grown in its sloping fields, and there's a wealth of other produce from apples (used for making cider and the distinctive preserve known as 'black butter'), to strawberries and the creamy milk from Jersey cows.

Seafood takes pride of place on the menu, from whole lobster to fresh oysters and buttery seared scallops, lip-smackingly good crab linguini or a tasty crab sandwich which you can tuck into sitting

Fresh crab claws

on a bench by the sea. Beef features widely, from sirloin to chateaubriand. You'll also find plenty of foraged ingredients making a show on menus. Increasingly, the choice of vegetarian and vegan dishes on the island is also increasing, from a token dish to whole tasting menus.

Given the proximity to France, just 14 miles (22km) across the water from the east coast, it is not surprising that Gallic dishes feature on menus. Firm favourites are *moules à la crème* (with Jersey cream, of course), *moules frites* or *plateau de fruits de mer*. There's also a strong pan-Asian influence in many restaurants – there are standout Japanese and Korean restaurants, and you're never far away from a good Thai or Sri Lankan curry. Of course, you'll also find familiar British staples like a big fry-up breakfast, Sunday roast, scampi and chips, or pots of tea that you can take down to the beach.

Jersey Royals are an island staple

Where to Eat

For a tiny island Jersey has a spectacular number and variety of restaurants. – from Michelin-starred fine dining to fashionable gastropubs, international cuisine to afternoon tea in a vineyard or the blissful simplicity of a crab sandwich bought from a kiosk on the beach, and eaten as you watch the sun dip lazily into the Atlantic. St Helier has the largest number and widest

ORMERS

If you happen to be on the beach from October to April during the neap tides, you might spot locals scouring the rocks at low tide in search of the near-mythical gastropod: the ormer. This indigenous mollusc, related to the abalone, can live for up to 15 years, and is prized for its unique flavour and mother-of-pearl inner shell. The Channel Islands are the most northerly of its habitats and it was once a staple of island dinner tables. Traditionally the shellfish were carried home in a basket, soaked, shelled, scrubbed, beaten with a steak hammer, browned in a frying pan, then cooked in a casserole with belly of pork, shallots and carrots. Overfishing led to the ormer becoming a gourmet rarity, and nowadays there are stringent regulations to protect it.

Fishing is only permitted between October and April, and only on the first day of each new or full moon and the five days following. This is the only time of year you are likely to find ormers on the menu.

range of places to eat, but there are great places to enjoy a meal across the island, including St Aubin, Gorey and St Brelade, to name just a few.

Eating out at lunchtime, you'll find many restaurants offer good-value two-course set menus. Hours are the same as those in the UK at lunchtime, but evening meals tend to be served earlier, especially at seaside restaurants where last orders are sometimes at 8 or 8.30pm. In summer it's usually wise to reserve a table in advance, especially if it's a warm evening and you want to dine alfresco.

Top 10 Things to Try

1. Shellfish

One of the biggest drawcards to eating out on Jersey is its fabulously fresh seafood, in particular its shellfish, much of which is caught locally. The clear, Gulf Stream-warmed waters around the island produce an abundance of shellfish including scallops, lobsters, chancre- or spider crabs, oysters and razor clams. The plump chancre crab is the most widely available but the sweeter spider crab is more sought after. Oysters, which used to thrive along the shores of the east coast, have seen a resurgence through farming at Grouville. Up to 600 tonnes of oysters are harvested here annually, making it the biggest production in the British Isles. The oyster seed is brought from hatcheries in France, then grown in netted sacks on the beach for around 18 months by which time they have reached their selling weight. Seventy percent are exported to the UK and France. Shrimps, prawns and langoustines on the other hand, a staple in many restaurant dishes, are imported, as are most mussels these days.

2. Fish

The fish most commonly seen in Jersey waters – and those which are the best to look for on restaurant menus – are sea bass (just called bass locally), bream (both black and gilt-head), brill, turbot,

THE JERSEY COW

The Jersey cow is known for its incredibly rich milk – perfect for making butter, cream, ice cream or clotted cream, the latter an essential indulgence which you can enjoy with Jersey cream teas. The handsome tan and white doe-eyed cows feature as watermarks on Jersey bank notes – as well as on numerous souvenirs from milk jugs to tea towels. The purity of the breed has been guaranteed since 1789 when a ban was imposed on the import of live cattle to the island. Since the end of the 18th century it has been exported worldwide and there is still high demand. India, Japan, New Zealand, America and Fiji are just a few of the countries where the breed can be found. Those watching the waistline or cholesterol level can always opt for the fat-reduced or low-fat Jersey milk, which is widely available.

Jersey bean crock

monkfish, skate mackerel and sole. In restaurants, look for the catch of the day which will usually be chalked up on a board – this is the fish most likely to have been caught locally, whereas fish like cod, salmon and tuna will definitely not be local. Note that local doesn't mean cheap – seafood prices are high, and if the fish is served by weight, check out what you're in for before giving the order. Jersey sea bass is becoming harder to find – a lot of what you see on menus is farmed elsewhere, and it's not a patch on the line-caught bass fresh from Jersey waters.

3. Jersey Ice Cream

Especially in summer, it's hard to imagine spending time on Jersey without indulging in some locally made ice cream, from the milk of the iconic Jersey cows. Best enjoyed on the beach, obviously.

Blanc Pignon, Soft Spot Gelato and Classic Herd are some standout artisan producers.

4. Jersey Royals

First propagated in 1880 and traditionally fertilised by seaweed, Jersey Royal potatoes have earned worldwide acclaim not only for their waxy texture and earthy, nutty taste but the fact that they are ready well before the earliest crops of new potatoes in the UK. If you happen to be in Jersey in April, there is nothing to beat the very first crop of the season, straight from the soil, and served with Jersey butter and a sprinkling of parsley.

Jersey Royals are grown on the island's steeply sloping fields or *côtils*, and have never been grown outside the island. They were awarded PDO (Protected Designation of Origin) status in 1997, and these days they account for half of the island's income from all agricultural products.

5. Jersey Vegetables

Aside from its famous potatoes, there's plenty of other fresh, locally produced fruit and vegetables on the island – strawberries, asparagus, broccoli, courgettes, peppers, tomatoes, carrots, shiitake mushrooms and more. You'll frequently see stalls with local vegetables and an honesty box beside the road – 'hedge veg' stalls, as they're known – you choose what you want and leave the correct change. Elsewhere, look for the Genuine Jersey Mark – the guarantee of local provenance, forproduce reared, grown and caught in Jersey (www.genuinejersey.je).

6. Jersey Bean Crock

Before the days of Jersey Royals, red and white beans were the island staples. They were grown on every farm on the island and it was the Jersey beans that inspired the Heinz baked variety – or so it's said. The beans were an essential ingredient of the hearty, cassoulet-like Jersey Bean Crock, cooked with pigs' trotters, belly of pork and onion and served with cabbage loaf, a delicious doughy gold-crusted bread baked in large cabbage leaves. The bread can still be found in some bakeries.

Jersey black butter for sale

7. Black Butter

The unappetisingly named Jersey black butter, or *le nier beurre*, is not butter at all, but a type of apple preserve used to spread on bread or toast. Islanders made this in enormous quantities in the days when the cider industry was flourishing, traditionally in a large copper urn where the ingredients – apples, sugar, lemons, spices and liquorice – were simmered in cider. The Jersey National Trust (www.nationaltrust.je) keeps the tradition alive, and if you happen to be in Jersey on the last weekend of October you can pitch in and help with peeling or stirring the pot in the bakehouse at The Elms, La Cheve Rue, St Mary. Black butter can be bought at La Mare Vineyards (www.lamarewineestate.com) or from Maison La Mare (www.maisondejersey.com) in St Helier.

8. Sweet Treats

Just occasionally you come across *des Mèrvelles*, or Jersey Wonders, which taste like doughnuts (without the jam) and are shaped in a figure of eight. Jersey housewives traditionally cooked them as the tide went out. They also cooked vraic buns, cakes made with yeast and raisins, and named after the vraic, or seaweed, which is collected from beaches and used as fertiliser. In days gone by families would gather to collect vraic from the beach, snacking on vraic buns (and swigging cider) between seaweed-collecting stints.

9. Cider and Wine

Cider was first introduced to the Channel Islands by the Normans and until relatively recently it was the main drink of the island. In the 17th century it was given by farmers to their staff to make up their wages. At the annual Cider Festival held at the Hamptonne Country Life Museum in October, you can watch traditional cider-making methods, with the apples being crushed and their juice extracted in a horse-driven, twin-screw press.

Jersey is pleasantly sunny, and shares the same degree of latitude as the Champagne region, so it's only natural the island should produce its own fizz. La Mare Wine Estate (www.lamarewine

CULINARY EVENTS

The island hosts a fast-growing number of foodie events, kicking off with the Spring Specials (mid-February to the end of March) when almost half the island's restaurants show off the best of their culinary skills and offer great-value set-price menus. Serious foodies should visit the island in late May during the week-long Food Festival, which celebrates the best from Jersey's food producers and chefs. The *Tennerfest* (six weeks from October to mid-November) is hugely popular; fixed price menus starting at £10 are on offer at 150 restaurants, including many of the best. At many fairs stalls sell everything from Jersey oysters to gourmet burgers. The Gorey *Fête de la Mer* in May is known for alfresco seafood dining; the *Foire de Jersey* features food stalls, French markets, and a Cheese Festival. October sees *Le Fais'sie d'Cidre* (Cider Festival), a lively event held at Hamptonne Country Life Museum to celebrate the island's heritage of apple cultivation and cider production.

A delicious cream tea

estate.com) is Jersey's only vineyard, and produces a sparkling wine – Le Murier, made from a blend of Seyval Blanc and Phoenix grapes – as well as a red, white and a rosé.

10. Gin

Jersey produces some wickedly good gins, from a young and imaginative bunch of small distilleries. Among the best are Sea Level Eco Distillery (https://sealeveldistillery.co.uk) run by Jersey's first female distiller, Sarah Gaudion – produced in small batches with an emphasis on locally sourced ingredients wherever possible, and using home-grown botanicals and recycled glass bottles. As the name implies, Jersey Cow (www.thejerseycowdistillery.com/home) make their gin from Jersey milk. La Mare Wine Estate (www.lamare wineestate.com) also make their own gin.

Places to eat

The price bands are based either on a two-course evening meal for one with a glass of house wine or for lunch where no evening meal is served. Prices exclude service charge, but are inclusive of the 5 percent Goods & Services Tax:

££££ = over £50
£££ = £30–50
££ = £20–30
£ = under £20

St Helier

Awabi 63 Halkett Place; www.awabi.co.uk. Excellent little pan-Asian restaurant, with good value small bites – Korean fried cauliflower, deep fired wood ear and shiitake mushroom wontons, and the like – and sharing plates along the lines of cumin lamb, crispy deep fried sea bass, or kimchi fried rice. **£££**

Banjo 8 Beresford Street; www.banjojersey.com. Converted from the Victoria Club, a private men's club next to the market, this is now part of the Jersey Pottery emporium. It comprises a stylish brasserie, a casual restaurant and an all-day café/bar, along with four chic guest rooms on the second floor. **£££**

Bohemia Green Street; www.bohemiajersey.com. One of Jersey's top gourmet restaurants is the Michelin-starred Bohemia, within the chic contemporary surrounds of the Club Hotel and Spa. Chef Callum Graham produces dishes such as aged Jersey angus beef tartare with braised short rib or pan-fried mullet with courgette and coriander, red pepper, harissa, and pickled cockles. **££££**

Café Jac Jersey Arts Centre, Phillips Street; www.cafejac.co.uk. Popular, good value and friendly café where you can turn up for breakfast, brunch and light bites any time of day, and enjoy globally-inspired full meals. Good choice of vegetarian dishes, takeaways available, tables outside. **£**

Cock and Bottle Royal Square; www.liberationgroup.com. Traditional pub with alfresco dining on the square (heaters and blankets provided); perfect for a sunny day to enjoy mussels and fries or pub favourites, with chilled wine or a beer. Inside, original 18th-century features have been retained. **££**

FOUR Artisan Bakery 53–55 Bath Street; www.fourbakery.com. Excellent little bakery and patisserie just around the corner from the Central Market, with delicious sourdough, pastries, cakes and sandwiches. **£**

The Fresh Fish Company Victoria Pier; www.jersey.com/see-and-do/fresh-fish-company. Savour a crab sandwich or lobster claw with a sea view or select fish from the retail shop to grill on a beach BBQ. The company supplies many hotels and restaurants with local fish. **££**

The Lamplighter 9 Mulcaster Street; www.jersey.com/things-to-do/food-and-drink/listings/the-lamplighter-real-ale-pub. The Lamplighter is renowned for its real ales, with five direct from the cask, plus ciders. This is a traditional town pub with wooden beams and working gas lamps, though not without its TV screens for watching the big games. Snacks and soup are served at scrubbed pine tables. **£**

Pêtchi Liberty Wharf; www.petchi.je/location. A wood-fired grill restaurant and wine bar inspired by the seascapes of the Channel Islands, with a nod towards the Basque Country. **££££**

Pizzeria Famosa 41 La Colomberie; https://pizzeriafamosa.com. Authentic Neapolitan pizzas. They also have a very good selection of vegan pizzas. **££**

Samphire 7-11 Don Street; www.samphire.je. A Michelin-listed restaurant delivering consistently high-quality cuisine in a stylish but relaxed setting. Along with set and à la carte menus, there's an excellent vegan menu. It offers all day dining options, and has two terraces for alfresco meals or drinks. **£££**

Tassili Grand Jersey, The Esplanade; www.handpickedhotels.co.uk/grandjersey/eat-drink. The opulent Michelin-listed Tassili restaurant, is located in the five-star Grand Jersey hotel. Chef Nicolas Valmagna's menus are inspired by his French heritage and love for fresh Jersey produce, and feature a selection of local ingredients. **££££**

Thai Dicq Shack Dicq Slipway, St Saviour; www.thaidicqshack.je. Bring your own bottle and chill on the sands with tasty, freshly cooked Thai cuisine. Try red snapper stir fry with lemon and ginger, Thai curry or plum and lemon ginger ribs. **£**

The Yard The Weighbridge; www.facebook.com/theyardjersey. This café is a good stop for brunch or a coffee beside the Jersey Museum and Art Gallery, offering breakfast plates, small and more substantial dishes, as well as cocktails. **££**

Bonne Nuit

Bonne Nuit Beach Café Bonne Nuit Beach; https://bonnenuitbeachcafe.co.uk. This inviting beach café has lovely views of the fishing harbour. Come for full English breakfasts, light lunches, seafood specials, crab sandwiches and classic Thai dishes using fresh local ingredients. Takeaway also available. The café is not licensed so BYOB. **£**

Gorey

Bass and Lobster Foodhouse Gorey Coast Road; www.bassandlobster.com. Chef Dave Jones is well-known for championing Jersey produce, whether it's hand-dived scallops, chancre crab or line-caught sea bass.

Despite the name of the restaurant there is always a choice of meat on the menu – again, mainly locally sourced – as well as vegetarian dishes. **££££**

Suma's Gorey Hill; www.sumasrestaurant.com. The little sister of Longueville Manor, Suma's is a small, stylish restaurant serving innovative British cuisine with emphasis on the best of Jersey's seafood. The sought-after seats in summer are those on the terrace with outstanding views of Grouville Bay and Mont Orgueil Castle. **£££**

Grève de Lecq

Moulin de Lecq Le Mont de la Greve De Lecq; https://moulindelecq.co.uk. The tavern is an ancient water mill with a stream that flows into the sea; it retains original stone and wood features and the main bar is built around the watermill's cog wheels and gearing mechanisms. The restaurant serves full meals and you can eat in the garden in summer. **£££**

Rozel

The Hungry Man Rozel Bay; https://thehungryman.je. This kiosk on the waterside is famous for its delicious crab sandwiches. You can sit at port-side tables with views of the bay, and walk along the pier for views of France on a clear day. **£**

St Aubin

enotèca Surrey House, Charing Cross; www.enoteca.je. Small Italian restaurant run by Jersey-born Kate and chef Marcello from northern Italy, championing local Jersey produce (including vegetables from their own garden), with an excellent selection of natural wines from Italy. **££££**

Lazin Lizard Charing Cross, Mont Les Vaux; www.lazinlizard.com. Buzzy little restaurant with tasty dishes such as crispy squid, bunny chow, sticky ribs and steak with teriyaki prawns. Fusion African-Asian-Caribbean with plenty of vegetarian options. Very popular – be sure to book. **££**

Lookout Beach Café First Tower, Victoria Avenue; www.thelookoutjersey.com. Between St Helier and St Aubin, with views across the bay, this café is a favourite among locals. Come for full English breakfasts, brunch (eggs Florentine or Benedict), afternoon tea, hand-made burgers, seafood platter or fish 'n' chips. **££**

Mark Jordan at the Beach La Plage, La Route de la Haule, St Peter; www.markjordanatthebeach.com. A casual bistro on the beachside promenade offering high-quality, simply-cooked cuisine with an emphasis on fish. The retro desserts like sticky toffee pudding are hard to resist. **££££**

Salty Dog Bar and Bistro Le Boulevard, St Aubin's Village; www.saltydogbistro.com. Stylish, laid-back eatery offering fusion cuisine, with food that is big on flavour, freshness and spice. A crispy aromatic duck salad might be followed by a whole roasted seabass or the sumptuous 'reef and beef' (seared scallops and king prawns with prime beef fillet in a chilli, garlic and coriander sauce), then a 'Gooey Jersey Black Butter & Banana Toffee Pudding'. Cocktails and contemporary music are part of the scene. **£££**

St Brelade's and Ouaisné Bay

Crab Shack St Brelade's Bay; www.jerseycrabshack.com. Landmark allday eatery with a terrace right on the bay, which began its life as part of a pottery shop across the island in Gorey Come for a light lunch or leisurely dinner and expect fresh local oysters, crab linguine, California-style fish tacos, and South Indian fish curry. **££**

Flavour Bay Café St Brelade's Bay, tel: 07829 996622. Apart from a great location right on the island's most scenic beach, this café serves excellent seasonal food prepared using local produce. Particular highlights include filling Japanese ramen and delicious organic juices. It's very casual – you can turn up straight from the beach. **££**

Old Portelet Inn La Route de Noirmont, Portelet; www.randalls-jersey.co.uk/the-portelet-inn. This huge family pub in an old farmhouse has a bar, bistro and lovely views of Portelet Bay. Play areas inside and out, live entertainment most evenings, piped music. **££**

Old Smugglers Inn Ouaisné Bay; www.oldsmugglersinn.com. These converted 18th-century cottages have real ales, log fires and a good range of pub food. House specials include slow-roasted lamb shanks with chive mash, and traditional fish & chips. **££**

Oyster Box St Brelade's Bay; www.oysterbox.co.uk. A stylish restaurant right on the bay, where you can move between ocean dips or beach games to a sumptuous platter of *fruits de mer*. Dishes along the lines of crab taglierini, and roast cod and king prawn curry, and there's a good choice of vegetarian dishes. The setting is contemporary, with fish-themed decor and alfresco terrace tables. **££££**

Portelet Bay Café Portelet Bay, tel: 01534 728550. Family-run café right on the beach with quirky upcycled decor. Delicious wood-fired pizzas, seasonal fresh shellfish, and salads. A lovely scenic spot, worth the trek down (no car access). Booking is essential in summer. **££**

St Clement

Green Island Restaurant Green Island; www.greenisland.je. The southernmost restaurant in the UK, Green Island has great sea views and outstanding seafood. The terrace overlooks Green Island itself. There is a casual beach café atmosphere and a long list of locally sourced seafood and you might find the likes of chancre crab salad, skate wings with caper butter or rack of lamb on the menu. **££££**

St Ouen's

El Tico St Ouen's Bay; www.elticojersey.com. This contemporary beach cantina, part of a surf shop and surf school, has great views of the surfing beach from its terrace and picture windows. The all-day menu caters for all tastes and ages: vegetarian mezze, gourmet burger, crab linguine and Mexican pulled-pork sandwich. **££**

Le Braye La Grande Route des Mielles; www.lebraye.com. Gaze across the huge bay of St Ouen's and stoke up on a big breakfast before a dip in the Atlantic. Or come for coconut prawn tacos, burgers, crab linguine, or roasted butternut squash salad. This is one of the safer areas for swimming at St Ouen's so it's very popular with families. **££**

Ocean Restaurant Atlantic Hotel, Le Mont de la Pulente; www.theatlantichotel.com. Dine in style in one of Jersey's top-end restaurants with breathtaking views over the gardens to St Ouen's Bay. Taste the finest and freshest from Jersey's coast and countryside – grilled Jersey seabass with couscous and artichoke hearts, roast new season lamb loin with crushed Jersey royals, crispy polenta gnocchi with forest mushrooms. **££££**

St Saviour

Longueville Manor Longueville Road; www.longuevillemanor.com. This beautiful country house hotel has a long-standing reputation for gastronomy. Meals are served in the elegant 15th century wood-panelled Oak Room or the bright and airy Garden Room. Chef Andrew Baird's cuisine is contemporary English/French, with the emphasis on Jersey ingredients. Order à la carte or go for one of the tasting menus (vegetarian and vegan versions of these also available) – dishes along the lines of hand-dived local scallops with chorizo and baby spinach, new season white asparagus with sweet red pepper compote, or deep water halibut with wakame, sea lettuce, and lobster tortellone. Impeccable service; extensive fine wine list. **££££**

Travel essentials

Practical information

Accessible Travel

For detailed information covering accommodation, transport, parking, attractions and equipment for hire for the disabled, visit www.jersey.com/holidays/accessible. The local Citizens Advice Bureau (www.citizensadvice.je) also has information on Jersey for the disabled. Specialist organisations which can assist with holidays include Enable Holidays (www.enableholidays.com/Jersey). On-street parking and public car parks have designated areas for UK and European Blue Badge holders. A shopmobility service operates from St Helier's Sand Street Car Park from Mon–Sat 10am–4.30pm April–October and 10am–2.30pm November–March (information at www.shopmobility.org.je). The Radar National Key Scheme operates in Jersey, and toilets with radar locks can be found in main centres and at most beaches. Visitors are advised to bring their own key, but they are available for loan (£10 deposit required) from ShopMobility Jersey. Special wheelchairs designed for beach access are available from the charity Beachability (www.beachability.org).

Accommodation

Hotel accommodation ranges from B&Bs, yurts and converted forts to country manor houses and luxury town hotels Top picks for luxury include the historic Longueville Manor Hotel (www.longuevillemanor.com) and the modern The Atlantic (www.theatlantichotel.com), while for glamping you can't beat Jersey Zoo (www.durrell.org/visit-jersey-zoo/stay-at-jersey-zoo). There are also a few hostels on the island, and plenty of self-catering options with good facilities. The accommodation section of the official Jersey website (www.jersey.com/stay) is handy for finding accommodation.

If you are going in July and August it is wise to book well in advance, especially if you require a room with a view. At other times of year there is little problem. Many hotels are closed from November to February. Some establishments will require a deposit or credit card details before confirming a reservation. A large number of hotels have special offers, such as three nights for the price of two or free car hire with three or more nights' stay. Booking online at some hotels can save you 10 percent.

Specialist travel agents for Jersey can organise tailor-made holidays with travel, transfers, insurance and car hire: try Channel Islands Direct (www.channelislandsdirect.co.uk).

Self-catering specialists include Freedom Holidays (www.freedomholidays.com) or Macoles Self Catering (www.macoles.com). For a holiday with a difference, you can stay at one of the beautifully sited fortresses, observation towers and follies that have been restored by Jersey Heritage (www.jerseyheritage.org) as self-catering accommodation. They include the red-and-white striped Archirondel Tower near St Catherine's Breakwater, the Barge Aground folly at St Ouen's, the German Radio Tower overlooking the Corbière Lighthouse, the Seymour Tower, La Crête Fort and Fort Leicester, both on the North Coast and an apartment in Elizabeth Castle.

Many visitors base themselves in St Helier, which has a good bus service to all parts of the island and is the starting point for island bus and boat tours. However, some of the smaller centres such as St Aubin, Gorey or St Brelade's Bay are far more picturesque, and have some excellent restaurants and good transport links.

Airport

Jersey Airport (www.jerseyairport.com) is located in St Peter, 5 miles (8km) west of St Helier. Taxis are metered and cost from £15–£22 from the airport to St Helier, depending on the location of your hotel – the taxi rank is immediately in front of the Arrivals hall. Four bus routes run between the airport and St Helier: bus No. 15 (via Red Houses and St Aubin, journey time 30 minutes), bus No. 12 (via St Aubin and St Brelade's Bay), bus No. 22 (express service, journey time 20 minutes), and bus No. 9 (via the Rugby Club, journey time 25 minutes). For timetables see the Liberty Bus website (https://libertybus.je). Tickets can be bought from the driver (cash or contactless) or using the Liberty Bus app. It's a flat fare of £3 for any journey on the island (£2.55 if using contactless or the Liberty Bus app).

Apps

Useful apps to have at your fingertips during your stay on Jersey include:
Jersey Taxi App www.jerseytaxidriversassociation.co/jersey-taxiapp.html

LibertyBus https://libertybus.je
PayByPhone (parking) www.paybyphone.co.uk

Bicycle Hire

For the energetic and eco-friendly, there is a 96-mile (155km) network of well-marked cycle routes, including Green Lanes where the speed limit is 15mph (24kmph). A cycling guide and map can be picked up from the Jersey Tourism Visitor Centre in St Helier and their website (www.jersey.com) gives details of bike-hire locations and guided bike tours. Try Lakeys (www.lakeys.co.uk) in St Helier, and Jersey Bike Hire (www.jerseybikehire.co.uk) in St Aubin.

Budgeting for Your Trip

The cost of flights from the UK vary hugely, from around £90 to £350 return, depending on the airline, time of year and day of the week (weekends are invariably more expensive). Hotel accommodation ranges from £80 for a double room in a basic guesthouse, £150 in a 3-star hotel and £200–£400 in a luxury hotel. Restaurant prices are similar to those in the UK. A pint of beer or lager is £3.25–£3.50; a bottle of house wine £8–£20; soft drink £1.45, cup of coffee £2–3; cycle hire from £16 per day or £50 a week.

Most attractions are free for young children and substantial reductions are given to senior citizens and students.

Camping

The island has several campsites, and reservations are advisable. There's the cushy **Durrell Wildlife Camp** at Jersey Zoo (www.durrell.org), which provides spacious pods with carpets, king-size beds, wood-burning stoves and outdoor decks with sunbeds as well as showering and kitchen facilities. You wake to the sound of lemurs or the sight of gibbons or red squirrels in the trees by your tent. Cooking equipment is supplied and the zoo has two cafés. There are additional teepees for children if required. Campers are allowed unlimited access to the wildlife park any time during their stay. Minimum stay is normally three nights. **Beuvelande** (www.campingjersey.com) in St Martin is the biggest campsite, with excellent facilities; the family-run, good-value Rozel Camping Park (www.rozelcamping.je) has views of France from one of its four fields and is within walking distance of the pretty harbour of Rozel, renowned for good restaurants. Both sites have a heated swimming pool and are only open from mid-May to September. Camping off-site is against the law and it is forbidden to pitch a tent anywhere on the island except on a designated site.

Car Hire

The minimum legal age to hire a car is 20 and there are varying maximum age restrictions. A valid driving licence is required, with no endorsements for dangerous or drunken driving in the last five years. Some companies impose an upper age limit. Car hire companies are plentiful and there is little difference in price between the international and local companies. A small car costs from around £58 per day or from £410 a week. Hire firms include:
Avis (www.avisjersey.co.uk)
Europcar (www.europcarjersey.com)
Hertz Rent-A-Car (www.hertzci.com)

All rented cars are branded with a large letter H on the number plate.

Climate and Tide

Jersey has the highest average number of sunshine hours in the British Isles, although the summer temperatures are no higher than those in some parts of southern England. In the summer months the island has a daily average of eight hours of sunshine and an average maximum temperature of 68°F (20°C). As in the UK, the best months to go are from May to September, the hottest months being July and August. High temperatures in mid-summer are tempered by sea breezes. The following chart gives the average maximum temperature for St Helier.

	J	F	M	A	M	J	J	A	S	O	N	D
°C	9	8	11	13	16	19	21	21	19	16	12	10
°F	48	46	52	55	61	66	70	70	66	61	54	50

The sea temperatures are refreshing for swimming, averaging 62.8°F (17.1°C) in summer. The island has one of the largest tidal movements in the world. During spring tides Jersey's surface area increases from 45 to 63 sq miles (72 to 100 sq km) and the vertical difference between high and low water can be as much as 40ft (12 metres).

Crime and Safety

Jersey is a safe place for a holiday but it is worth taking all the usual precautions: always lock car doors and don't leave your valuables unattended. Dial 999 for police, fire, ambulance or coastal rescue services. Report a loss or theft to the police within 24 hours if an insurance claim is to be made.

Driving

Jersey has the highest ratio of cars to people of anywhere in Europe, and around 36 percent of car trips on the island are less than 2 miles (3km). St Helier is notorious for traffic jams. Elsewhere driving is relatively stress-free, but beware of the very narrow lanes in the countryside, many of which are used by tractors, cyclists and pedestrians. Given these narrow lanes and the maximum speed limit of 40 mph (64kmph) there is no point in bringing or hiring a high-performance car – although a remarkable number of islanders seem to own them. Despite its small size the island has more than 350 miles (563km) of paved roads. You may lose your way in the rural interior but it won't be for long. Signposting is reasonably good and you are never very far from a village or beach resort.

Visitors bringing their own car to Jersey by ferry must have an insurance certificate or International Green Card, a vehicle registration document, valid driving licence or International Driving Permit.

Rules of the Road. Rules reflect those of the UK: driving is on the left; seat belts are compulsory for adult front seat passengers, children must wear belts or a suitable child/infant restraint in both front and rear seats; it is an offence to hold a mobile phone while driving. Fixed alcohol limits and road-side breath testing are similar to the UK. Penalties are severe, with up to a £2,000 fine or 6 months' imprisonment for the first offence plus unlimited driving licence disqualification.

The maximum speed limit on the island is 40 mph (64kmph), reduced to 30 mph (50kmph) or 20 mph (32kmph) in built-up areas and 15 mph (24kmph) on Green Lanes where priority is given to pedestrians, horses and cyclists. Yellow lines across roads at intersections indicate 'Stop and give way'. A single yellow line along the length of the kerb means parking is prohibited day or night, and is liable to a fine. The 'Filter in Turn' system, whereby vehicles from each direction take it in turn to cross or join the traffic from other directions, is used at some of the main junctions. Traffic lights in Jersey change from red to green with no amber in between.

In the event of an accident or breakdown call the police (tel: 999) who will advise the best course of action.

Parking. Parking is paid for through the Pay by Phone app (www.payby phone.co.uk) which also includes a location of car parks across the island.

Electricity

The current is the same as that of the UK, 240 volts AC, with British-style three-pin sockets. Visitors from other European countries will need an adapter; those from the US also need a transformer.

Embassies and High Commissions

Australia Australian High Commission, Australia House, The Strand, London WC2B 4LA; www.uk.embassy.gov.au.

Canada Canada High Commission, Canada House, Trafalgar Square, London SW1Y 5BJ; www.international.gc.ca.

New Zealand New Zealand High Commission, Kinnaird House, 1 Pall Mall East, London SW1Y 5AU 4TQ; www.mfat.govt.nz.

Republic of Ireland Irish Embassy, 17 Grosvenor Place, London SW1X 7HR; www.ireland.ie.

South Africa South African High Commission, South Africa House, Trafalgar Square, London WC2N 5DP; https://dirco.gov.za/uk.

United States American Embassy, 33 Nine Elms Lane, London SW11 7US; https://uk.usembassy.gov.

Emergencies

In an emergency, dial 999 for police, fire, ambulance or sea rescue.

Getting to Jersey

Jersey Tourism (www.jersey.com) provides comprehensive information on air and ferry services from the UK. Year-round package holidays, either by sea or air for short or longer breaks, can be arranged through British and local tour operators. Specialist operators include JerseyTravel (www.jerseytravel.com) and Channel Islands Direct (www.channelislandsdirect.co.uk). Alternatively most of the hotels, guesthouses and self-catering establishments on the island can arrange travel for you, as well as travel insurance and car rental if necessary.

By Air

A dozen scheduled airlines and numerous charter operators service the island from over 30 destinations across the British Isles, plus airports in mainland Europe. Off season the number of flights is reduced, especially from regional airports. From the UK the main low-cost operator is Easyjet (www.easyjet.com) which flies from from Belfast, Birmingham, Edinburgh, Gatwick, Glasgow, Liverpool, Luton and Manchester. British Airways (www.britishairways.com) operate regular flights from Gatwick and Heathrow. Other airlines flying to Jersey include Jet2 (www.jet2.com) and Blue Islands (www.blueislands.com). Auringy (www.aurigny.com) flies from several destinations in the UK and France to Guernsey, but not to Jersey. The best prices are normally secured by booking well in advance. When booking with low-cost carriers watch out for all the hidden extras. Prices vary considerably according to the time of year.

By Sea

After 60 years of operating ferries between the UK and Jersey, Condor Ferries handed over the reigns to DFDS in 2025. DFDS (www.dfds.com/en) now operate direct sailings year-round between Jersey and Portsmouth, Pool and Saint-Malo. Condor (www.condorferries.co.uk) run ferries between Jersey and Guernsey (year-round, journey time 2 hours on their Commodore Clipper or 1 hour on Condor Voyager), and from Guernsey to Saint-Malo. Islands Unlimited (https://islands-unlimited.com) operate a fast catamaran service between Jersey and Guernsey (May–September, journey time 60 minutes), while Manche Îles (www.manche-iles.com/en) runs services between Jersey and Guernsey as well as Sark, and between Jersey and Granville (all April–September).

Jersey's Elizabeth Harbour ferry terminal is a 10-minute walk from the bus station, and there's a taxi rank outside the terminal building. In 2024 plans were approved to redevelop the Elizabeth Harbour ferry terminal, with work beginning in 2025.

Guides and Tours

Tantivy Blue Coach Tours (www.tantivybluecoach.com) is a long-established, reasonably-priced coach and tour operator offering all-day or half-day tours. Jersey Bus Tours (www.jerseybustours.com) operate two different tours in vintage open-top buses, departing daily April to September from Liberation Square. Hopper tickets allow unlimited travel on both routes.

Health and Medical Care

Apart from treatment solely within Jersey's A&E department, visitors have to pay for medical services and treatment. This includes emergency hospital treatment (such as operations) not within A&E, repatriation, out-patient appointments, GP visits and prescriptions. Australia, Austria, France, Guernsey and Alderney, Iceland, New Zealand, Norway, Portugal, Sweden and the UK have reciprocal care agreements with Jersey which cover emergency hospital treatment; however, the agreement does not cover certain types of follow-on treatment or travel costs. Visitors are therefore advised to take out comprehensive health insurance or check that their existing policy covers travel to the island. Check online for information on Covid-19 requirements and restrictions at www.jersey.com/plan-your-break/general-information/healthcare/covid-19-information.

The General Hospital at The Parade, St Helier, JE1 3UH (tel: 01534

442000) has a 24-hour emergency unit. The majority of GP surgeries provide a service for visitors. Jersey Tourism can provide a leaflet with the details of island surgeries. Medical prescriptions can be dispensed at any of the island pharmacies.

Tap water is perfectly safe to drink.

Language

English is spoken throughout the island but has only been the official language since the 1960s. The island's tradition is French, and even today some French words are used by the court and legal professions. In St Helier and other parts of the island you will see some street names in French, occasionally with the contemporary English names alongside. On rare occasions you can overhear some of the older residents speaking in Jèrriais, the local patois based on Norman French. Until World War II this dialect was widely spoken, with true French used to conduct written business. Local societies are anxious to keep the historic dialect alive; there are occasional pieces in Jèrriais in the *Jersey Evening Post* and the language is taught in some schools.

LGBTQ+ Travellers

Jersey only decriminalised homosexuality as recently as 1990, but today the general attitude of islanders towards LGBTQ+ visitors is not so different from that in the UK. Same-sex partnerships on the island have been recognised since 2012 and there is a small, friendly LGBTQ+ scene on the island. Liberate (https://liberate.je/for-visitors) is a good resource for LGBTQ+ visitors to Jersey.

Money

English sterling is freely accepted on the island, as are UK cheques and all major debit and credit cards. Jersey issues its own banknotes (including a £1 note) and coins, which have the same value as sterling – and this is generally what you'll be given in change when on the island. However Jersey notes and coins can only be used in Jersey, not in the UK – so aim to either spend this on the island, or you'll need to go to a bank or Post Office when you're back in the UK to exchange it for sterling (notes only, not coins).

ATMs are widespread throughout Jersey. For currency exchange, banks generally offer a much better rate than *bureaux de change*. A few shops accept euros.

Opening Hours

Banks. Banks have similar opening hours to those in the UK, with some open on Saturday morning.
Shops. Normal opening times are Mon–Sat 9am–5.30pm. There is no general Sunday opening in Jersey but the shops at Liberty Wharf, St Helier, and a few convenience food stores remain open. The markets and some shops are closed on Thursday afternoon.
Tourist Attractions. Most museums and tourist attractions are open from April to October; some are also open March to November, daily 10am–5pm, though the times are subject to change. Jersey Tourism can provide a list of current opening hours, or you can telephone them to check times for specific sites.
Pubs. Most pubs are open Mon–Sat 9am–11pm, Sun 11am–11pm.

Police

In an emergency dial 999. The police headquarters are at La Route du Fort, St Helier, JE2 4HQ (tel: 01534 612612; www.jersey.police.je/s). Along with the regular police Jersey has a network of honorary police officers who don't wear uniform.

Public Holidays

Jersey has the same public holidays as the UK with an additional day's holiday on 9 May, Liberation Day, commemorating the end of the German Occupation in 1945.
1 January New Year's Day
March or April Good Friday and Easter Monday

First and last Mon in May Spring Bank Holidays
9 May Liberation Day
Last Monday in August August Bank Holiday
25 December Christmas Day
26 December Boxing Day

Public Transport

Bus

Jersey has an efficient, easy-to-use network of buses, operated by LibertyBus (www.libertybus.je). All bus routes radiate from the Liberation Station, St Helier. Bus timetables, with a map of the routes and a Liberation Station layout plan, are available online or free from the bus station. For details go to the LibertyBus website. You can also text the bus stop code (shown beside the bus stop) to 07797 798888 to find out the arrival time of the next bus. Bus tickets cost £3, which is a flat fare wherever your destination on the island.

If you're getting two buses for the same journey, get a 'transfer ticket', which costs the same but will be valid on both (however it's only valid for 1 hour). You can buy tickets on the bus, but the best way is to download the LibertyBus app. Discover Jersey passes allow unlimited travel for 1, 2, 3 or 7 days and are available from the driver or from the bus station. These are also available as family passes (valid for two adults and three children up to the age of 15). Summer services from mid-May until early October are far more frequent than those off season.

Taxi

Taxi ranks are only to be found at the airport, the arrivals building at the harbour and in various locations in St Helier. Rates vary according to the time and the day. Extra charges are made for waiting time and luggage carried in the boot. The Tourist Office has a list of taxi companies at www.jersey.com/plan-your-break/getting-around-jersey/public-transport-taxis. These include Citicabs (https://citicabs.je), Domino (www.dominocabs.je)

and Yellow Cabs (www.yellowcabs.je). Ryde (www.ryde.je) have a fleet of electric vehicles.

Le Petit Train

The little tourist trains departing hourly with on-board commentaries are fun for families (www.littletrain.co.uk). They operate daily from April to October, between Liberation Square, St Helier and St Aubin. You can also board the train in West Port.

Telephone

The UK telephone code for Jersey is 01534. When dialling from outside the UK preface the code by 44 (for the UK) and omit the 0. STD codes for the UK from Jersey are the same as those used from the UK. As in the UK, international calls can be dialled direct from any public phone.

Mobile Phones. Beware that Jersey does not work on the UK system and there can be high charges for making and receiving calls on a UK mobile. Prices are set by the relevant UK service provider and, as the UK networks do not extend to Jersey, these are usually costed as international calls. The three main Jersey networks are JT – which has the best coverage, Airtel-Vodafone and Sure. The network extends to the other Channel Islands. Visitors with mobiles will either be linked automatically to a network or can select the network manually.

Some pay as you go phones do not function in Jersey so check with your provider before you go.

Time Zones

As in the rest of the UK, the Channel Islands are on Greenwich Mean Time (GMT), with clocks moving forward in late March, and reverting back in late October.

New York	**Jersey**	Paris	Jo'burg	Sydney	Auckland
7am	**noon**	1pm	2pm	11pm	1am

Tipping

Tip as you would in the UK. In restaurants service is often added to the bill, in which case there is no need to tip.

Toilets

There are clean public toilets at main sites and at most beaches. Cafés are usually laid back about the public using their facilities, although if you buy a drink it will be appreciated.

Tourist Information

The Jersey Tourist Information Centre (www.jersey.com) is located at Jersey Museum, The Weighbridge, St. Helier, JE2 3NG. The office has free maps and can arrange accommodation as well as provide tourist information on the island. It is open all year, daily 8.30am–1pm and 2–5pm.

Visas and Entry Requirements

Although a passport is not necessary for visitors arriving from the UK, airline passengers will need valid photographic ID in order to travel, and a passport is required for onward trips to France. Other EU citizens require passports.

New immigration rules were introduced in April 2025. European (non-UK) passport holders traveling to Jersey via the UK now need an **Electronic Travel Authorisation (ETA)** before reaching the UK border (an ETA costs £10, valid for multiple visits over two years, and is usually approved within three days). This does not apply to those traveling to Jersey direct from mainland Europe, either by ferry from France or arriving by air. More details on visa requirements on the GOV UK website at www.gov.uk/check-uk-visa.

As Jersey is not a full member of the European Union, you can still purchase duty-free items when travelling to and from the island. Maximum allowances are: 200 cigarettes or 250gr of other tobacco products; 1 litre of spirits or 4 litres of sparkling or fortified wines and 4 litres of other wines; 16 litres of beer or cider; 60cc/ml perfume; 250 cc/ml eau de toilette; £390-worth of other goods (watches, jewellery, cameras, etc).

Websites and Wi-fi

Wi-fi access is available at the airport, Jersey harbour lounge, Liberation bus station and most hotels and cafés.

Here are some popular websites:

www.jersey.com The official Jersey Tourism website is packed with information and should cover all your needs, from how to get there, where to stay and eat, to transport, sports, activities and events. It is easy to use and gives interesting background information as well as all the practical details.

www.islandlife.org This is the largest community website serving the Channel Islands.

www.jerseyeveningpost.com The local paper with the latest Jersey news, weather, what's on and tides

www.jerseyheritage.org Details of all the Jersey Heritage sites to visit on the island and information on holiday lets in some of their quirky historic properties.

www.libertybus.je Everything you need to know about the Jersey buses.

www.nationaltrust.je Jersey's National Trust. If you are a member of the UK National Trust make sure you take your card when you go to Jersey. The Trust is the largest private land owner on Jersey, and is dedicated to preserving sites of historic, aesthetic and natural interest. Admission is free for NT members on production of a membership card. The organisation has a year-round programme of guided walks and events.

Index

MINI JERSEY

Second edition 2025

Editor: Siobhan Warwicker
Author: Rudolf Abraham
Picture editor: Piotr Kala
Picture Manager: Tom Smyth
Cartography Update: Katie Bennett
Layout: Danielle Titmas
Production Operations Manager: Katie Bennett
Publishing Technology Manager: Rebeka Davies
Head of Publishing: Sarah Clark
Photography Credits: All images Mockford & Bonetti/Apa Publications except: Andy Le Gresley Photography/Seymour Hotels 16T; iStock 16BL; Shutterstock 1, 9, 12, 15T, 15CT, 15B, 18T, 18CL, 18BR 18BL, 20T, 20CL, 20BR 20BL, 26, 28, 33, 72, 82, 103, 115
Cover Credits: Rocks and flowers **iStock**

About the author

Rudolf Abraham is an award-winning travel writer, photographer and guidebook author. He is the author of over 15 books and has contributed to many more, and his articles are published widely in magazines. www.rudolfabraham.com

Distribution

UK, Ireland and Europe: Apa Publications (UK) Ltd; mail@roughguides.com
United States and Canada: Two Rivers; ips@ingramcontent.com
Australia and New Zealand: Woodslane; info@woodslane.com.au
Worldwide: Apa Publications (UK) Ltd; mail@roughguides.com

Special Sales, Content Licensing and CoPublishing

Rough Guides can be purchased in bulk quantities at discounted prices. We can create special editions, personalized jackets and corporate imprints tailored to your needs.
mail@roughguides.com
roughguides.com

EU Representative

LOGOS EUROPE, 9 rue Nicolas Poussin, 17000, LA ROCHELLE, France; Contact@logoseurope.eu; +33 (0) 667937378

Printed by Finidr in Czech Republic

ISBN: 9781835292426

This book was produced using **Typefi** automated publishing software.

A catalogue record for this book is available from the British Library

Contact us

Every effort has been made to ensure that this publication is accurate, free from safety risks, and provides accurate information. However, changes and errors are inevitable. The publisher is not responsible for any resulting loss, inconvenience, injury or safety concerns arising from the use of this book. If you notice any errors, outdated information, or potential safety risks, please send your comments with the subject line "Rough Guide Mini Jersey Update" to mail@roughguides.com.